The Diaries of William Brewis of Mitford

1833-1850

Transcribed by
Joan Foster & Dr Michael Smith

Edited by Hilary Kristensen

The Diaries of William Brewis of Mitford 1833-1850

First Published November 2007
by Wagtail Press
Gairshield
Steel, Hexham
Northumberland
NE47 0HS
www.wagtailpress.co.uk

ISBN 978-0-9538443-8-2

Designed by T.W.Kristensen

Printed and bound by Robson Print Ltd. Hexham

CONTENTS

ACKNOWLEDGEMENTS

The William Brewis diaries have been made available by permission of Dr. Melanie Wood, Special Collections and Archives Librarian, Robinson Library, University of Newcastle Upon Tyne.

Many thanks to Irene Straughan and Brian Laverick of the Mitford Historical Society.

We would like to thank the following for giving permission to use these images and photographs: Frank Addison, Print Services, Robinson Library, University of Newcastle Upon Tyne: pages 6 & 7 Photographs of Brewis diary pages. Beamish Museum, Regional Resource Centre: Front & back cover images from an agricultural employment poster , photo no. 161917. Northumberland Collections Service, Woodhorn: pages 20 & 21 (NRO 4267-1-2 plans 2 & 3), pages 36 & 99 (NRO 0876-345 – McLeod Collection), page 92 (NRO 0876-387 – McLeod Collection). Engravings on pages 43 & 63 – Border Antiquities of England & Scotland 1812; page 79 – Grose's Antiquities 1775. Pages 14, 33, 45, 73, 102, 106, 109 - Thomas Bewick woodcuts. Page 116 – illustrations by W.H.Pyne

---

Descendants of Thomas Brewis

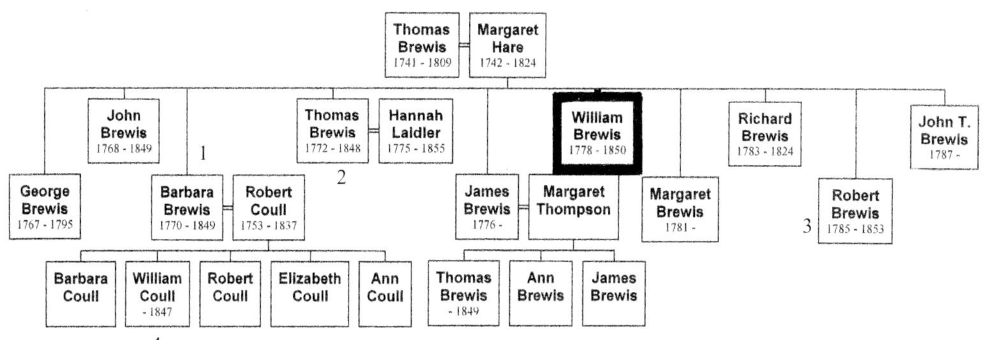

Frequently mentioned members of William's family:

1. Barbara known as "Sister Coull".
2. Brother Thomas
3. Brother Robert
4. Nephew William

INTRODUCTION

William Brewis's diaries were first brought to my attention by Dr. Michael Smith and Joan Foster, who had discovered these rare records of early 19th century rural life, in the Robinson Library Special Collections at the University of Newcastle Upon Tyne.

Joan Foster discovered the Brewis diaries whilst doing research into the working lives of rural children in the 19th century for an historical thesis. Until the increasing demands of the thesis took over, Joan selected and transcribed numerous entries from the handwritten diaries and published articles about William Brewis. At a later date she made contact with one of William's descendants – the successful writer Henry Brewis. Although Henry was aware of the existence of his ancestor's diaries, he sadly died before he could visit the library. The fact that William and Henry both wrote about rural life in Northumberland is particularly interesting.

Dr.Michael Smith found William's diaries whilst delving into his family history; he was surprised and delighted as his great great grandfather was a Brewis. Hoping he had found a family connection, he discovered that William never married but was part of a large family. The diaries soon became a compulsive read and he spent many hours transcribing further extracts, absorbed by William's accounts of local, national and international matters. Michael eventually found that he is William's second cousin five times removed!

William Brewis was clearly a man of some social standing. He was an Overseer for the Poor and a High Constable for the West Division of Morpeth in addition to being a respected farmer. His diary entries give the reader a fascinating insight into social, family and political events, farming, fairs and markets, weather, crops and livestock, hunting, horses and hounds etc. The diaries also include William's outspoken judgements upon national contemporary celebrities.

I am extremely grateful to Joan and Michael for transcribing the following extracts from all fifteen of the diaries which span the years 1833 – 1850. Due to their hard work we are all now able to enjoy these rare first-hand accounts of rural life in the first half of the 19th century.

William's original spelling and grammar have been retained.

Hilary Kristensen

Editor

3d. Week. JANUARY 13, to 31 Days.

DATE.	ACCOUNT OF CASH.	RECEIVED.
	Brought forward £.	

The great Topick of Conversation is the Queens Wedding, which is said to take place about the middle of next Month, in Feb.y, with Prince Albert of Germany of the Gotha Family of very poor extraction, but England is expected to provide His Excellancy with a suitable Income as a consort of the Queen of England say 50,000 (Generous England) you pay very dearly for your follies, but then he is a protestant Prince, tho part of his family are Catholics, we have been in the habits of getting our Kings & Queens from Germany (as much as to say the pure Blood,

Carried forward £.

31 Days.	JANUARY 19, 1840.	1st. Month.

PAID.	APPOINTMENTS, BILLS DUE, &c.

M. 13. Died at this place Thomas Rutherford aged 70 a Cottager under me.

Tu. 14 Sold 26 Ewes on Turnips to Mr. Brunton Morpeth at 27/= each, say 14 d per Quarter

W. 15. A full Market of Stock, Beef 6/6 Mutton 6 to 7. per ~~lb~~

Th. 16. A blowing day, but still it is favourable for Plowing.

F. 17. Sr. Matt. White Ridleys Hounds at Middleton Bridge, a very fine day

Sa. 18. A hard Frost but Plowing at afternoon Land is getting dry

Su. 19. A Stormy, blowing sort of day, several Showers of Rain.

Carried forward

William's farmhouse at Throphill Hall Farm

Previous pages – two pages from William's diary for January 13th – 19th 1840

1833

January 1
Here my friends, we are just entered again upon another New Year!!! Struggling against debts, taxes, tithes and feudal impositions, these are trying things. Nevertheless let us not despair for the horizon of our hopes may at times be overcast, as it has been hitherto. Yet I hope oppression and misrule will in the end do good, to make us humble and pray to Almighty God that he will be pleased to guard us through the labyrinths of this wicked world and bring us to that haven of bliss, where when troubles shall cease and be carried into the arms of our Redeemer. When the Great Judge of the World sitteth to judge us according to our works, and god grant that we may be prepared to meet that awful day. Amen !!!

January 1 -6

The Dutch Troops have evacuated Antrip and the French & English have taken possesion of the Citadel…

Sun. 6th — A very severe frost and has the appearance of a continuance. The Rev. W. Yarker at Mitford preaches a charity sermon in aid of the Free Schools today

January 7-13

The state of the country at this time is most alarming, particularly the farming interest. The 'gift' as it is called in the wheat crop is not half that we generally ought to have and the prices are so low. The best price for wheat is 11/- to 12/6, oats 3/6 to 5/-, barley 6 to 7/6, beans and peas, 6/- to 7/6. The price of land must come down the one half, indeed farms are to let all over the county. Seizures and failures likewise are very common but still nothing to what they will be in the spring when the rent becomes due in May.

Thur 10th — A fine frosty morning burning whins and thorns off the land where oats is to sow.

January 14-20

Great expectations is depending upon this Reform, that is now for the first time introduced into this country. Earl Grey has now begun with the pruning hook to top off several of those useless places and pentiones that have so long infested the county and I hope he will continue doing the same until everything can be done consistent with the security of the State.

January 21-27

A great number of farms to let all over the county and really the prices are so very bad that the farming interest is not worth following.

Fri 25th_ Still frosty and no plowing. Had Humphries, Police, Morpeth, paying a visit to detect muggers and gypsies, to keep them from doing mischief.

Mon 28th Loading coals. W Thompson Newcastle here with Brother Robert. Fine sport with greyhounds, killed two hares and dined at Newton Park.

January 28-February 3

The state of Ireland is very alarming in respect of being so agitated by the O'Connell. Nothing but a repeal of the union seems to be the wish of the Irish. The Catholics and Protestants and Whiteboism all disagree and plunder of firearms and murders are committed all over the country.

Sat 2nd Sold 22 bolls wheat @ 11/6 to 12-13-0. A very bad market, I do not know what will become of the Corn Farmers.

Mon 4th My berth day (sic) but no spice cake or yet brandy.

February 4-10

...expedition in search of Captain Ross and his brave companions, left England 3 years ago and has never been heard of since.

Wed 6th A full market of cattle. 6/- for the best and 6½ per lb (?) for sheep. Turnips – plentiful.

Sat 9th Delivering 45 bolls barley to W. Johnson, Newcastle making altogether 180 bolls @ 8/6

Tue 12th All hands ploughing for oats. Fine season and the lands work well. We will expect the seed times will commence next month.

Thur 14th Benj.n Bullock Esq, Mr Joseph Fenwick, Thriston, Brother Robert & Charly Robson Greyhound Coursing little Sport, Dined here & spent the afternoon.

February 18-24.

The corn trade is still in a depressed state, the farmers will be all knocked up. The spring rents will never be got.

Mon 18th Northumberland hounds at Ponteland.

Tue 19th Looking at Harnham Low Hall Farm for Brother Robert, 89 acres, we think worth £100.

Sun 24th Brother James here today & set off to Grange Moor on the afternoon. I set him as far as Hartburn.

February 25-March 3

Trade of all kinds is very bad and no likelihood of being any better.

March 4-10

There has been shipped from London this year for Van Deamon's land 600 females to assist to populate that province.

Wed 6th Hinds Hiring, great number of servants. Those hired for money was lower, but Corn allowance was the same.

March 11-13

Fox hunting, Pigdon banks, Meldon Park

Sun 24th At Hartburn Grange Moor to dinner with Brother James of Blyth...

March 25-31.

The land is in such a wet state and neither the beans and peas or oats could possibly be put in.

Tue 26th Brother James here from Blyth…

Wed 27th Morpeth Horse Fair, a great number of all kinds of horses.

Sun 31st At Mitford Church Revd. Luke Yarker Vicar

April 29-May 5

The markets grow daily worse. I do not know what will become of the county without the landlords should take it into consideration. If not the game must be up.

Wed 1st May Morpeth Fair, for the hiring of single servants. I engaged one man, 25 years of age at 11 £, 6 £ for the Summer and 5 £ for the Winter.

Sun 12th Geo. Brewis here from Angerton and Brother Robt from Newton Park.

Tue 21st Our rent day at Mitford. Paid ½ year rent, due Martinmas, £152

Sat 25th Shearing sheep, the wool is likely to be a good price.

May 27-June2

We have had rent day on the 21st and have got a new Steward called Thos Tindall. What has happened our late man Mr Pepper time will try, between the two they have taken me in completely. I was ordered last May by Mr P to pay the Masons, Joiners, Slaters etc which I did in the beginning of June & have lain out of my money until now & when I come to settle for my Rent left me to pay Lime, Stones, Hair, Laths, part Timber altogether about 20 £. I was foolish enough to send my Rent in Full last Martinmas by order of Mr Pepper. Therefore I have been left in the lurch, which is a great shame now when times are so bad, all Gentlemen are making Handsome Returns & I pay out of my own Pocket for other Gentlemens Property.

Mon 27th — At Rothbury Fair bought a calving cow, £10~15~00, a very fair market, sheep scarce.

Sun 9th Jun — ....Brother James and daughter & Robert, Newton Park here to dinner. A dull day. I have rheumatism in my right knee.

Tue 11th — Mrs Thompson set off to dine at Thornton along with my niece Ann Brewis, Blyth, but thunder, lightning and rain.

June 24-30

The wool trade is considerably better... the woollen manufacturer is giving much higher wages, which is a little glimmering hope that times are upon the advance. Week sowing Turnips

Thur 4th Jul — Stagshawbank Fair

Sun 7th — Brother James here from Blyth on his road to Grange Moor

Thur 11th — All hands at piking hay, put up 46 pikes in good condition, but the weather is not very bright.

July 8 – 14

Mr Davidson Vicar of Hartburn Died on the 6th Inst about 80 Yrs he has left a Family of one Son & 3 Daughters to a former wife, the present Wife now Living is a Barren Widow who is left the Interest of 250 £ & the one Half of his Furniture, the other part goes to Frances, who Married Mr Clint of Stanton, now at Harnham, Agent formerly to Sir Charles M Monk of Belsay Castle and is retired upon his means. The Vicar has been very extravagant during the early part of his Life, part of the living has been confiscated for upwards of 20 Yrs therefore he has been in very low circumstances during the latter part of his lifetime, a fine Old

Gentlemanly sort of Man and very pleasant company to spend the Evening, 'pleasant and kind'.

July 22 -28

Brother James' son Thomas of Blyth has had the misfortune to be shipwrecked on the Banks of Newfoundland in a ship called the Wellington belonging W. Heron, Blyth bound for Quebeck with stores and merchandise upon the 10th May was beset with icebergs some 50 miles long, had about 10 passengers imigration to that province with the intention of making their fortune a large piece or field of ice stove in their bows and was a total wreck in half an hour, they lost everything and was taking on board by a Sunderland vessel and their lives saved unexpectedly for thick fog was all around them, at the time, and fortunately this vessel hove in sight and saved their lives.

[*For his holiday in August, he walked to Blyth and bathed in the sea early and late each day.*]

Sun 4th Aug	Bathed this morning at Half past 6 very cold. Sea high North wind, at Bridge End Meeting, and Balast Hill in the afternoon very religious.
Wed 7th	Set off on foot from Blyth this morning at 9 o'clock, rested an hour at Guide Post, dined at Green's Bridge, Morpeth. Got home 4 o'clock.
Tue 20th	Sold 6 Oxen to Mr Jessee Graydon Butcher Sunderland
Wed 21st	Sold 11 Oxen to Mr Jessee Graydon…
Sun 25th	At Mitford Church Hearing Rev Luke Yarker and a very bad preacher indeed.
Sun 22nd Sep	I am going to Grange Moor this morning. Brother Thos. has got a protruberance cut from the back part of the head, big as a hen's egg.

Week 41 Oct 7 - 13

A strange appearance in the Heavens something like the Northern Lights but I never saw any thing like this appear'd Saturday evening 12th all the Heavens were lighted all over but the North particularly just like as if the Northern Hemispere was all on fire…

Sun 3rd Nov Wind from the North, Stormy and cold, not at Church. Mitford Church very cold and little entertained.

Sun 15th Dec To Dine at Newton Park with Mr Ephraim Dixon, Morpeth & Nephew R. Coull.

Sun 22nd At Grange Moor this afternoon visiting brother Thomas & family. All well but complains of the times like everybody.

Mon 23rd Had our Association meeting at Mitford. 25 members attended the whole consisting of 34 meetings(?) . I being Secretary and Treasurer made me a very throng day. We are allowed 2/6 for dinner & 2/6 for liquor and a fine of 2/6 for every member that does not attend. We engage Robert Humphries, Police Morpeth to attend once a month to disperse all muggers and disorderly person that is encampt upon the publick highway, likewise to assist in apprehending any depredations that is likely to be committed in any of our premises.

Thu 26th Cold and very frosty had Brother Thos & James here all day.

Published in Bell's Life, London

A mate of a ship called *Hornsby* took a dose of of Hydroceanic acid to produce pleasurable excitement and he died - too much at once!!!

Whig administration
Taxes taken off annually – £6,235,000
Lessened the expences – £3,471,000
Official Person's salaries - £259, 200
Abolished places 2000- £369, 250
Ministers, Chancellors etc £199,430
Ambassodors etc £50,525
£10,584,435

A saving to the country since Earl Grey came into office and still people say that the Whigs has done nothing after fighting their way through all classes of the community.

The following farms to be let at May-day next 1835, belonging to the Dean of Kirkley, Savil Ogle Esq.

		Acres	R.	P
Saltwick	W.Hall	879	1	22
Broad Law	Codling	403	1	6
Shilvington	G.Codling	308	3	39
Start up	Hedley	258	0	6
Watch hill	Cowle	246	2	10
Ogle Castle	Coull	488	2	24
Bonas Hill	Jones/James(?)	253	2	16
Ogle South	Ellison	188	1	27
Tod Hill	Temperly	230	2	19
West Newham	Robson	348	0	0
Dam house	Buckham	250	1	0
Carter Moor	Owner	188	1	38
Kirkley March	Bewick	176	0	0
Kirkley Mill & Farm	Coxon	58	1	4

Apply to Mr Wm Grace, Saltwick, near Morpeth

Again my friends, we have just seen another year pass the confines of time into the unfathomable gulf of Eternity, which brings us upon the stage of 1834 and from what I saw, the New Year is likely to be fraught with many important events, especially as regards the political state of this and some other countries. We are still in the midst of troubles and vexations, brought on by profligate Wars, which has intailed upon us a ruinous debt, the interest of which, if not speedily removed, bids fair to destroy the vital energies of the Nation. Eight Hundred Millions in solid cash!!!

1834

Wed 1st	New Years Day, begins with open weather, and the people are for most part very dull owing to the badness of the times!!!
Thu 2nd	A great party of us at Thornton to dinner and tea. Spent a very agreeable day, Mr. Coull was in great spirits, and was glad to see us all, about 15 in number.
Fri 3rd	All hands at the plow. The weather is very open for the season of the year. It would be more conclusive for the health if a little frost and snow at this season
Sat 4th	Sold 40 bolls of brown wheat at Newcastle to Mr Brown at 11/3 = 22-10-0. A dull market, prices low.
Sun 5th	Rain this morning. The weather in general is very open, no appearance of snow or frost as yet!

Week 2 January 6-12

A great number of farms in the newspaper all over the County to let and I should think they should be much reduced in value, if according to the present prices of grain. I think there ought to be a premium for bad land given for industrious Tenents, if the expences is taken off for cultivation upon poor soils not growing more than 8 bolls per acre. The expences of working and manure will balance out the income. Grass lands have been paying rather better, wool and stock has upon the whole been selling fairly.

Mon 6th	The North'ld hounds at Bolam. Killed at Angerton Moor, after a very short run. Rain.
Tue 7th	Attending a sale of stock at Bradford, belonging to Sir Charles M. Monck, by distress. Rain!!
Wed 8th	A full market of all kinds of stock, best beef 5/6, mutton 5 ½, Rainy day.
Thu 9th	Rain, very disagreeable weather, the plows are going but nothing but wet.
Fri 10th	Still Rain, day and night never ceases. The plows are going

Sat 11th — Rain, I never saw a greater continuance of wet weather.

Sun 12th — Dull kind of morning and been Rain last night. The land is bottomless, no looking out.

Week 3 January 13-19

The Winter so far has been very open without frost or snow, the wheat is looking very rich and luxurious, too much so, at this season. My bad land in the moor is as green as it should be in the latter part of May. I seldom saw a good crop of wheat, when looking so flush at this time. Frosts generally comes early in the spring and crops all that superabundant often makes tender after. But looking at the present prices, we ought not to think or look forward, for the difference between good and bad cannot make much difference.

Mon 13th — Wet and unhealthy weather. Mr Coull here all day, making a good crack!!!

Tue 14th — Mr. Bell, gamekeeper at Nunriding, is turned off for mismanagement this morning.

Wed 15th — Rain, Morpeth a full market of stock, prices a shade lower, beef 5/6, mutton 5½

Thu 16th — Still Rain and wet. Expected to thresh a stack of wheat but must continue. The weather is so wet. At Mr. Bullock's to dinner

Fri 17th — A stormy wet morning but the plows are going. John Rees here for Newcastle market.

Sat 18th — Very windy this day all hands plowing leas for oats. We have had no frost or snow as yet.

Sun 19th — John Reed here from Newcastle market yesterday. He says a bad market. Oats he got only 3/6 and some he saw only 3/3 and sold some wheat at 9/6, a poor look out for farming.

Week 4 January 20-26

I was at Newcastle market last Saturday 25th and sold to Mr Nox 40 bolls wheat, weighing 8st 9lb - 10/3 and really I never saw the market so bad and the people so down in their spirits, and the oats no better prices. I saw some as low as 3/-. The best potato oat at 4/6 and what the event will be remains only to be seen in the future, because it is impossible that people can make any rents much less to make expences. The wheat market was small only two rows. I have seen twice as much at this season, but it appears there is great arrivals from all places.

Week 16 April 14 - 20

Great disturbances all over England, France & Germany, the People's minds are set against all the governments. The English tradespeople are forming unions... ...The Parisians do not like Louis Philip as King, there has been a great deal of bloodshed at Paris and Lyons and would like to have a Republick Government. The French are a very unsettled sort of people, they do not know really what they want.....

Sat 11th May [*The Star Coach overturned in Percy Street, Newcastle and many passengers were injured.*]

> I happened to be outside behind and was thrown down with my foot under the iron rails of the coach and got my foot severely bruised. [*He was on crutches for some weeks.*]

Tue 3rd June Brother James here from Hartlepool paying a visit among us.

Mon 1st Sept Very ill this morning. Sent for Dr Hawdon at 2 o'clock.

Week 36 Sep 1 - 7

I have had severe illness from cold. It first seased my head on the right side and after that the ear throat and neck. I have been all blistered over the head and temples, have been leached in five or six places for fear of brain fever. I at one time thought of nothing but distraction, my head was all pained over, the most excrutiating pains, my head with pain is all in small lumps like Pidgeon Eggs. I thought at one time that the scull would be torn asunder. The doctor says it is like that filthy disorder called tic dolloro but considerably worse than any he had ever seen.

Week 37 Sep 8 - 14

I continue still very ill, my head is broke out in blotches on the back part and runs all over, a kind of lea still the pain continues I can scarsely stir from my seat.....

Sun 14th Very unwell today Oblidged to send for Doctor Hawdon for the violent pain in the Head. Apply'd 10 Leaches.

[*He was ill for about a month (more gory details!) but slowly recovered.*]

Week 39 Sep 22 – 28

My Health improves very quickly. I have been able to walk out this morning 28th but oblidged to return on acct. of the wet!!!

Tue 23rd — John Thompson Meldon Kill'd yesterday, a stone fell upon him in the Quarry.

Week 40 Sep 29 – Oct 5

Married at Coldstream by Especial Licence, W. Ephraim Dixon, Wine Merchant, Morpeth, to Elizabeth Coull, daughter of Robert Coull Esq, Thornton, my niece on or about 21 September and was Married over again at Morpeth Church on Monday the 29th Sept. She Eliz was paying a visit at Mr Reeds, Birness near Jedburgh & Mr Dixon taken the opportunity of going in a Post Chase and taken her away to Coldstream, unknown to either Father or Mother makes it very dissagreeable to pairent however such things has been done before & likewise may be done again.

Tue 7th Oct — Sold 10 Oxen to Mr Jessee Graydon, Sunderland
Sold Mr Graydon 9 Sheep at 30/=. Prices of Stock good.

Fri 7th Nov — A tremendous wet day, no looking out. Brother Robt. here detained on his road to Harnham.

Sun 16th — I have to Dine at Newton Park to meet Mr & Mrs Thompson Newcastle with the Bride and Groom Mr & Mrs Dixon Morpeth.

Sun 23rd — A fine Frosty Morning. No Stock taken into the Folds the weather is so favourable.

Mon 1st Dec — Taking the Cattle into the Folds for the first time. I seldom knew being so long!!!

Mon 15th — Mitford Association, 30 members, I being chose Treasurer, had to act in that capacity.

Sun 21st — Brother James here to spend the Christmas. A very fine day with bright sun.

Thu 25th — Christmas Day had all my Friends to Dinner the Weather being so fine, they enjoyed themselves.

Fri 26th — St Stevens Day Mr Mitford's Beagles here today running some Hairs but fue kills.

Most classes of his most gracious Majesties subjects complain of bad Government now the Tories have got into office, I am very doubtful we shall be governed the same as we have hitherto been under the same Laws and Constitution, the Bishops, Clergy and the Pentioners.

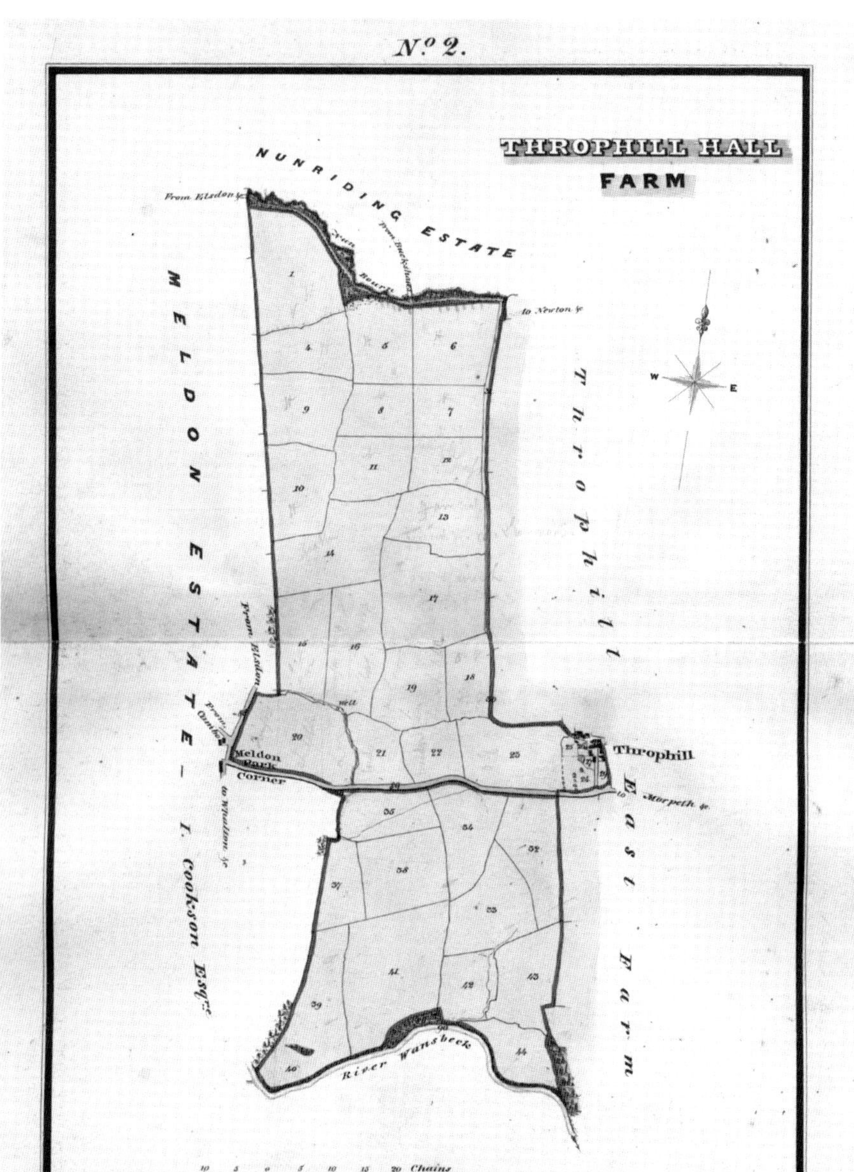

Plan of Throphill Hall Farm 1839

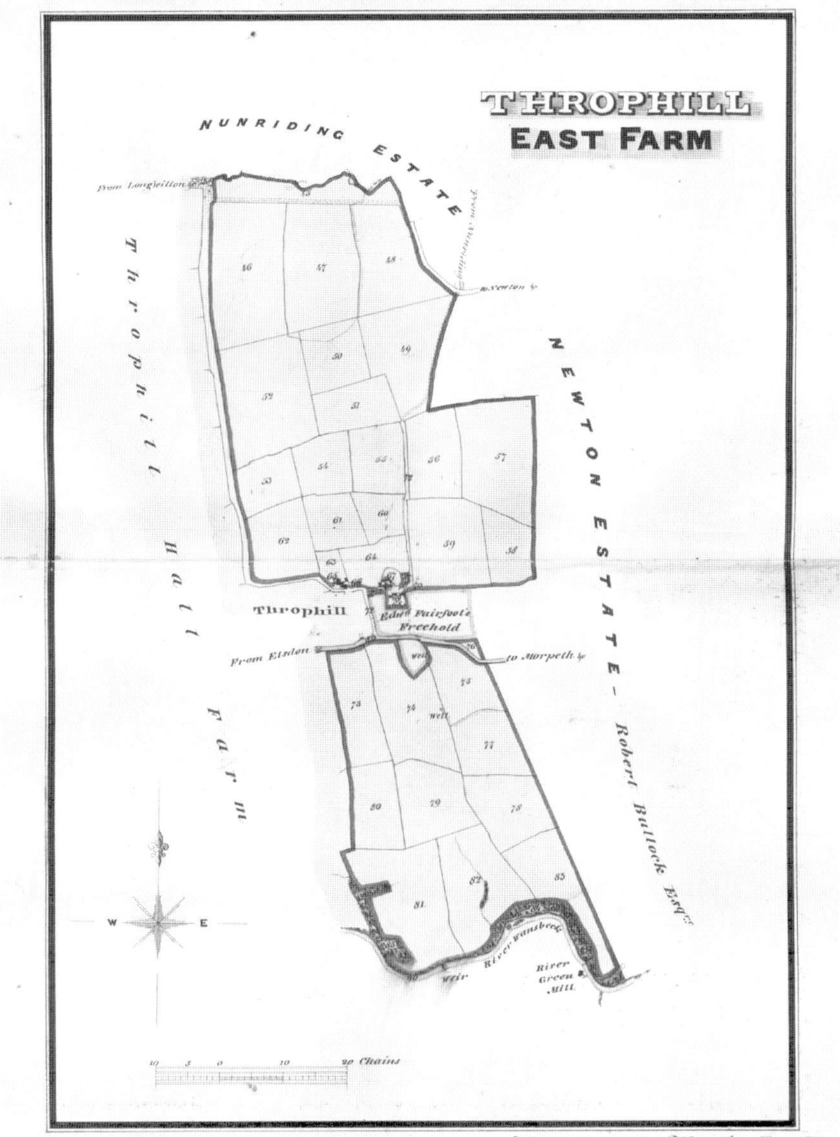

Plan of Throphill East Farm 1839

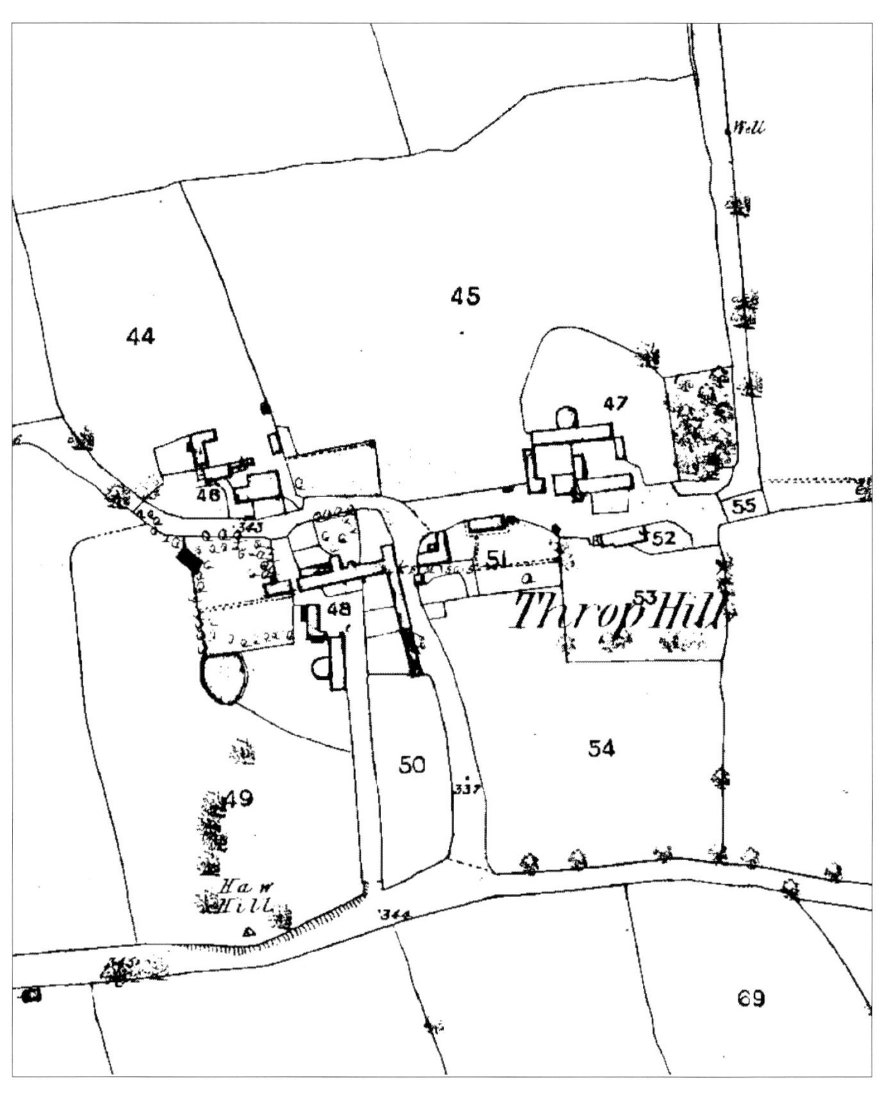

By 1895 the two farms appear to have been amalgamated

1837

The year begins very stormy and all covered with snow. Dismal accounts are received from all parts of the Country particularly from the south, all over the southern Counties and particularly west of London. The snow in many places is 8 and 10 feet thick. The coaches and other stages have been less or more stuck fast and in many places two and three coaches together. In one place three coaches were left not far from a cottage where they remained for two days but fortunately the poor people had the day before killed a pig, which made up for the predicament.

Sun January 1st
We now come to the first day of January 1837. The ground is all covered with snow and intensely frosty. Still we like to see plenty of Winter, which this season has just come in time to our wishes, but how it may answer time only can unfold. But for those few seasons back, the weather at this time has been in general open, which we attribute to bad corn and grass years. But however this has been the strangest season ever can be remembered.

January 2-6

We anticipate better times for the farmers. The prices for all produce is upon the advance.
Wheat – 13 to 14/-
Oats – 5/6 to 6/-
Barley – 8 to 9/-
Beans and Peas – 8 to 10/-
Beef – 5/6 to 6/6 per st (?)
Mutton - 6 to 7½
Veal – 7 to 8/-
Pork 6 to 7/-
Which upon the whole are very fair prices provided the seasons were favourable not like last harvest.

Mon 2nd	Deep snow and the roads are all blowing up. Coaches are stopped.
Tue 3rd	There are some cattle past for tomorrow's market but they have had to take the fields.
Wed 4th	A better show of stock at market than could possibly be expected. Beef @ 6/6
Thu 5th	All the cattle and sheep are to be fed from the effects of the snow.
Fri 6th	A kind of thaw this morning but preparing for Newcastle.

Sat 7th	Sold 40 bolls wheat at Newcastle, Mr Davison at 13/6, a full market.
Sun 8th	A frosty morning, the snow is all bratted, makes the sheep get to the ground badly.

January 9-15

What a strange season this has been now, when the frost has been so severe people would have thought that all diseases would have been buried in the snow. But hold, there is an epidemic all over the land and scarce a person is without some severe indisposition; some in one way and others in another. This that is affecting all this house the doctor calls influenza. I have not been out of the house for more than a week, my eyes are all closed up this morning.

Mon 9th	A great fresh and the snow goes quickly off. The waters are very big.
Tue 10th	All covered fresh with snow. It had been a tremendous fall last night.
Wed 11th	A full market at Morpeth, beef 6/6 and mutton 6½.
Thu 12th	At Morpeth, meeting the auditor for the books for the Morpeth Poor Law Union.
Fri 13th	A kind of thaw but the snow goes very slowly away.
Sat 14th	Stormy and frosty, the snow is unwilling to quit the hedges.
Sun 15th	I am very unwell, which every body has a little of illness, called influenza!

January 16-22

Died this day 17th Newcastle James Morton Esq. Married my neice, An Coull of Thornton. He has been a very clever man has been for many years the sole manager of the Grand Allies Collieries both in the Wear and the Tyne. A Gentleman possessed of great qualification. Cashier of all the workman, paid all the Laws and other affairs. He has left my neice Ann without children, but I should expect comfortable. He has £300 yearly beside House, coals and candles etc.

Mon 10th	I had the Doctor today and I feel myself very unwell. Bled etc.
Tue 17th	Brother Thomas has paid me a visit and spent the day, hearing I was unwell.
Wed 18th	My eyes are almost totally closed up this morning from inflamation. Ellen [*William's housekeeper*] had gone to Morpeth.
Thu 19th	Brother Robert was here this morning. A kind of thaw.
Fri 20th	My eyes are still much inflamed but I think they get a little better.

Sat 21st	A kind of raw frost this morning and likely to be a fall.
Sun 22nd	A dull morning and a great fall of Rain at afternoon.

January 23–29

Great meetings all over the country, some Tories and other Whigs. Sir Robert Peel, the great Tory, has been at Glasgow and made a long speach inflaming the people to return to Tory principles and Lord Morpeth this last week advocating Whig principles just as much the contrary. I should think that many of them are mostly for places and pensions, more suitable than advocating any of their principles; the loaves and fishes are the grand climaterick.

January 30-February 5

Died at Thornton on Thursday morning, sincerely regretted by all his old acquaintances, Robert Coull Esquire of 84 years of age and possessor of North Middleton Estate and occupier at this time. A man possessed of strong mind and great quallifications. About the year 1788 or 1789 he married my sister Barbra, who is at this time living at Thornton under severe indisposition from an applophic fitt and is benumbed on one side and not likely to get better.

Mon 30th	At Mr Robert Coull's funeral today, at Thornton, a good old man 84 years old.
Thu 2nd Feb	A great greyhound course at Ogle for a silver cup and a snuff box. Mr Armstrong, Newcastle, first.
Sat 4th	Died this morning old James Rodgers, aged 93, a shoemaker.

February 6-12

A great number of farms are let all over the country at an advance of rent and there appears to be great competition who shall be the Tenent when Proposals are taken, which has been too much the case. I am very sorry to say, as it is a very blind way of taking a farm. Perhaps you are bidding against yourself and perhaps against a worthless chap that has not a shilling to loose and in where the prospect is at this time to be better. I cannot see, unless it must be the stock.

Mon 6th	The finest day we have had for a long time. At the funeral of James Rodgers.
Tue 7th	All hands plowing to get forward with the oat land. Most of the people is back
Wed 8th	A very full market at Morpeth, beef @ 6/6 to 6/9, mutton 7s per stone.
Thu 9th	Threshing wheat, a tolerable fine day, better than could be expected.
Fri 10th	A thick, muggy day. Hartburn Village, Mr John Boag Huntsman?

Sat 11th	Rain and a very disagreeable day, the plows were obliged to leave off at eleven
Sun 13th	A very cold and stormy appearance, very unsettled like weather.

February 13–19

The greatest number of Deaths ever was known all over the Country from this Epidemic complaint called the Enfluenza, particularly among the old people. The newspapers are filled. There are more dead from this complaint than the Cholara, so called. This has been more like the Plague than anything else. The old people of my acquaintance have all gone, indeed it has been very severe upon the young likewise. It has scarsely passed any, even babes.

Mon 13th	Rain, no person can look out, but it rather faired at 12 and they got to the plow.
Tue 14th	Valentine Day, a tolerable fine day for the season, but wet underfoot.
Wed 15th	A full Market of stock. Beef at 6/6 to 7 ½ per stone, mutton 7 to 7 ½ .
Thu 16th	At Wingates Moor seeing Mr Thomas Reed, a drizzly day not much rain.
Fri 17th	A dry morning. Northumberland Hounds at Northgate, from there into Pigdon Banks.
Sat 18th	Delivering 28 bolls barley to Mr Linox Callerton for seed @ 9/6.
Sun 19th	A gloomy morning, looks like nothing but rain.

February 20–26

The season still continues as severe as ever. This morning it is frozen as hard as a stone wall and the wind north. It will make many look forward to save the hay and straw, being very little upon the ground last summer and then the awkward wet season that there was to little to begin with, and so very badly got, the hay particularly was a very bad crop. In some places it is now at 8 d. per stone and £7 per ton, which is considered very high. But if the season does not naturally improve I do not know what the consequences may be.

Mon 20th	Threshing wheat, a kind of stormy day.
Tue 21st	Northumberland hounds at Edington, found a fox at Rivergreen Whin.
Wed 22nd	Beef 6/6 to 7/-, mutton 8/- per stone, a full market of beef but sheep dear.
Fri 24th	All laying white with snow, the season rues? nothing it has done.
Sat 25th	A frosty morning, no plow can go. The wind north and very cold.
Sun 26th	A severe frost. All as hard as a wall, with a little snow upon the ground.

February 27-March 5

This complaint that has been going the rounds all over the country still continues, commonly called influenza. It still has left behind a kind of weakness and debility and many people that were severely held have not got strong again. In France they are as bad. I saw a letter from Isabella Milburn last week from Paris. It appears they are equally as bad as here. She gives sad accounts of Louis Philip, the present Reigning King of France, that he can scarsly be seen out of doors without a Guard being constantly with him.

Mon 27th	Newcastle Assises. The morning is favourable. Threshing Hopetown oats.
Tue 28th	A dull day has the appearance of rain. All hands plowing stubble.
Wed 1st Mar	The hinds hiring, bondage wages a little higher, 9/- small work and harvest, 1/6
Thu 2nd	At North Middleton with brother Greyhound Coursing, killed six hares.
Fri 3rd	A wet disagreeable morning but the plows are going.
Sat 4th	Sold 60 bolls of Hopetown oats to Mr Clark, Grand Allies Collerys @ 6/9
Sun 5th	A frosty day and very cold wind, North, but the land appears drying

March 6-13

The Hinds hiring commenced on the first day of March at Morpeth. They through the course of the winter have been meeting and forming a kind of Union amongst themselves not to bind their wives or maids to what is commonly called bondage. It has made a great stir throughout the county, in many places, say Alnwick, Wooler, Rothbury, etc. They got to open violence, knocked the farmers down and tore the Caps of them saddly, but at Morpeth they were more quiet, the only difference was in the wages of the women. – say 9 & 10d per day and harvest 1/6.

Mon 6th	A beautiful day, all hands spreading Lime upon the Turnip land.
Tue 7th	A very frosty day the land will scarcely plow but still we like to see dry.
Wed 8th	A bright frosty morning, plowing Turnip land for sowing with barley.
Thu 9th	Very unwell of a violent head ache, from cold. Delivering 29 bolls wheat to Mr Blair.
Fri 10th	A very stormy day, wind and Rain from the west, rather better today
Sat 11th	Delivering 60 bolls Hopetown oats to North Middleton. R.Coull, Esq., @ 7/-Snow laid.

Sun 12th — A very frosty morning with a part snow lying upon the ground, will keep the spring back.

March 13–19

Most of people are beginning to cry out for want of fodder. The winter has continued so long and the season has been so very severe since October 29th last year. We may say it has always been a fall of snow or rain up till this day, 17th inst. The hay was light and bad quality to begin with and then the straw was badly got, consequently then must have a great deal of waste and the winter setting in so very early that it cannot be wondered at. I should think the young wheat must suffer very much, it being so very badly put into the ground.

Mon 13th	A great fall of snow this morning. It is laid 1 foot thick, no husbandry work forward.
Tue 14th	Wind north and very frosty, the weather-glass quite set to fair and every appearance of wintery weather.
Wed 15th	An overflow of cattle and sheep at Morpeth today and as may be expected prices lower.
Thu 16th	Sent Mr W. Crawford Trewick 60 bolls Hopetown oats for seed at 7/-, a very good sample.
Fri 17th	Still a stormy winter. Since October 29 last year it has been continually some fall of snow.
Sat 18th	Cold and north wind. The weather appears unsettled.
Sun 19th	All covered with snow and the wind north-east. George Brewis here from Angerton to dinner.

March 20-26

Such a season as this has never been seen by the oldest person living. On the 29th October last year it was a complete drift of snow all day, Newcastle Fair Day. I got 20 bullocks and had some difficulty to know them after I had purchased them for just at 12 o'clock the drift was so bad that it was very bad to know them. But before that the season was very bad and so much Corn all over the fields. Now even to this day 26 Easter day it is no better, snow and frost. The people to the west of here expect nothing but to loose all their sheep stock. There are some already have suffered so much as 20 score, where there are large parcels (?).

Mon 20th	All covered with snow. The season looks dismal. It has been bad since 29th October
Tue 21st	Still frosty and stormy, no appearance of better weather. Threshing oats for seed.
Wed 22nd	A very full market of cattle at Morpeth and the prices lower, 6/6 mutton, plentiful supply.
Thu 23rd	A stormy day and still more snow, quite drift from the north-east.

Fri 24th	Good Friday Still snow and very stormy, the ground is all covered.
Sat 25th	A severe frost and like nothing but snow, no plows can go. A female child born last night, Abraham Scott and Matilda.
Sun 26th	Snow, Easter Sunday, a severe frost since the 29th October, we have perpetually nothing but change, but mostly snow.

March 27-April2

Great quantities of stock appears at market, from the Turnips running out. Morpeth on Wednesday last, was a great number than was wanted and prices gave way a little and sheep was plentiful likewise.

Beef the best price 14 per lb. 6/6 p st.
Mutton 6/-
Veal 7/-
Lamb 30/- each
Pork small pigs 4 6/-
Wheat best 14/-
Oats best 6/8
Barley 8/6
Peas 9/-
Beans 9/-
Rye 8/-

Mon 27th	Easter Monday, Morpeth Horse Fair, a very stormy day, perpetual snow.
Tue 28th	Frost and snow, such a season never was seen. Every day snow, sheep and cattle will be lost.
Wed 29th	Snow and frost and no likelihood of being any better, fodder is scarce.
Thu 30th	One of the borrowing days, still falls of snow every day. Ewes lambing, bad weather.
Fri 31st	Still falls of snow with a severe frost, such weather never was numbered.
Sat 1st April	A severe frost and several showers of snow. No chance of seed time.
Sun 2nd	A frosty morning. Ewes lambing, we have got nine, they appear to be quick.
Mon 3rd	A tremendous snow storm all day, the Ewes & lambs we have them in the houses & places.
Tue 4th	Still snow and the wind north, the oldest man living never saw such weather.

Sun 23rd	A tremendious Rain & has been all night all the fields are flooded & I do not know the consequence. Like the year 1816 on

April 25, a cold Rain from the NE completely laid all the land under water and the crop following was very bad.

Wed 3rd May Morpeth Fair for Servants, men very high. I hired 2 men 14 & 17 £ and one girl 8 £ per year.

Fri 12th The great flitting day for married servants. The roads were filled all day.

May 15 - 21

The weather continues very bad, up till this time May 15th there is no grass and the young wheat you can scarsly see any upon the ground. I still have all my cattle in the House & Holds and I have only two carts of Turnips left consequently they will have to take their chance. Tomorrow will have to be the day for a total turn out, for all kinds of stock and the grass is so short that it is only fit for sheep, the Oxen will never get themselves filled. The Oats is just beginning to appear upon the ground.

Fri 2nd June A dry cold day but the Spring is bad, no grass. Cheviot Hills is covered with Snow.

I had my neice Mrs Stobert from Picktree in County Durham spent 2 days with me in her Carrage and servants. I have not seen her for 17 years. I was glad to see her, she is a friendly well disposed woman.

June 12-18

Died on Friday morning Mr Thomas Vint of Newton Mill and an old staunch parishioner, who I believe to be a very honest man, aged 87 years as they say. Has left three daughters and one son Thomas, whom the charge of the mill and ground will fall upon to assist his aged mother, who is very lame and not able to look after anything. I am very doubtful he has been much distressed in mind on account of the mill being stopped all winter, with the great flood in December that took away the head dam and the men are now repairing it, but he has been doing nothing all winter.

Mon 12th All hands plowing the Turnip land, to be ready next week to sow.

Tue 13th The weather has changed a great deal for the better, clipping sheep 3 hands.

Wed 14th A full market of stock beef 8/-, mutton 7. A good many cattle, bullock, Scotland.

Thu 15th	A beautiful day all hands preparing Turnip land. The Rain yesterday has done good.
Fri 16th	A beautiful day. Corn and grass grow quickly. How long has the country been barren.
Sat 17th	Been a fine Rain last night will do good with warmth. At Wingate Moor last night.
Sun 18th	A very dull day, with a little rain from south-east. There is wonderful improvement in both grass and corn this last week.

June 19-25

Died at Windsor the King of Great Britain, William Henry, the third son of George the 3rd, born 21st August, 1765. He served as a midshipman on board a man of war in the West Indies, in Nova Scotia and after that he was under the command of Lord Nelson, who was recommended by that gallant officer. I had the pleasure of seeing him on my road from Windsor to London about 5 years ago. He appeared to be a round faced good looking man and very plain. He has been a good King for this country.

June 26-July 2

Princess Victoria proclaimed Queen, daughter of the Duchess of Kent. The nation being unanimous for the young Queen, it is expected she will follow the precepts of her Uncle William, the 4th who has been the best king that has reigned in England for centuries before. I had the pleasure of seeing him on my road from Windsor just 7 years on July 7th. He appeared to be a stout good looking man, no ostentation, no pride, no show but plain sailor like was W. the 4th.

July 3-9

The funeral of King William the 4th takes place on the 8th, Saturday at 6 o'clock in the evening. There is a covered way laid from the Palace to the Royal Chapel, the same as when I was at Windsor at the death of George 4th in 1830. It must have been great expense to the nation, the tons of deals laid all the way, that two carriages might pass each other. Besides the interior of the Chapel Royal was all laid with deals and covered with black cloth of the very best quality. The remains is laid in a vault where many of the Royal Family sleep in death.

Sat 8th	The King's funeral at Windsor at 6 o'clock. The shops partially closed at Newcastle.

July 10-16

A severe thunderstorm both Friday and Saturday 14 & 15 and we hear that some sheep being killed at Greenlighton and the windows all broken at Harewood Gate. It continued through both days with severe falls of rain and the fire was most awful. I was out on the moor on Friday afternoon about 3 o'clock and the fire and thunder fell both together fell just where I was and I was stupified and turned quite round. When I looked round I saw my bloodhound dog standing upon his hindlegs looking with astonoushment to know what was become of me. I at the time being stupified and deaf did not know what I was about.

Mon 10th	All hands leading Lime from Belsay, Greenlighton and Stanton, fine dry weather.
Tue 11th	I had Mr Graydon from Sunderland who bought 10 oxen near 60 stone for £20 each and £5 return.
Sun 16th	A fine morning, Mr Thompson's 2 sons left to go home after the midsummer vacation from Dr. Bruce's Academy, Newcastle.

July 17-23

Parliament is broke up after the death of William the 4th. The young Queen Victoria in person dissolved both Houses with a very pretty Speach she at 18 delivered. Her mother, the Duchess of Kent, is a very fine woman and bears a most excellent character and a most liberal disposition. We still hope that the Reform will be carried forwards the young Queen declares herself a liberal. The present Ministers still continues in office, Lord Marlborough still holds the highest place in the State with the rest of the Liberal Ministry. The Tories are down in their stirrups!!!

July 24-30

The awful and sudden death of a near relation of ours at Shawdon Wood House happened with that great thunderstorm on the 14th &15th of this present month to Miss Barbara Donkin, Mr Donkin's only daughter and neice to Ralph and John Carnaby, who are own cousins to us. The electric fluid had entered the west room chimney and gone through into the kitchen along the bell-wire where Miss Donkin was sitting, adjusting some part of her dress and was knocked down and her hair set on fire, and two dogs killed likewise at the same place, most awfull visitation!!!

Fri 13th Oct	This is the beautifullest weather that I ever seed at this season. The weather glass is at set fair.
Sun 15th	A serene fine day the Clouds very high, we had an Eclipse in the Moon on Friday night. The Moon was all over hid at 11 o'clock at night with a clear sky.

Nov 13 - 19

Died at Shawdon Wood House Mrs Donkin of a broken heart. She never could get her spirits up after the Death of her Daughter who was kill'd by lightning on 15 July last and being the only Child & her two Brothers living single with her, they likewise are much distressed & John it is reported is in a very poor state. They two Ralf & John Carnaby are our own cousins & are both single men & must be about 60 years old. I should gladly like to here of them getting better, two fine men.

Sun 19th Nov Geo Brewis here from Low Angerton to Dinner.

Dec 18 - 24

We had our great meeting of the Mitford Association on the Monday 11th Inst at the House of Mr Robt Thompson, the Plow Inn, consisting of 31 members, the most liberal Association in the Kingdom, we pay 5/= entrance & the expenses never has run to more than 7/= per year. I am the Treasurer, we have been fortunate not many convictions we hire a police from Morpeth & pays him 4 Guineas a year to be at any of the Members call at one time and to appear at one Moments Notice without a name being signed to the Order.

Sun 17th Dec A beautiful morning at this Season. The Season is most wonderful such as we seldom has seen in late years.

Tue 19th Preparing the Mitford Association to be gazetted in the Chronicle and Hue & Cry Newspapers.

Tue 26th A beautiful day at this season. W Thompson & Brother Robt greyhound corsing at North Middleton with R Coull Esq.

1838

Fri 19th Jan	Taken very ill of a severe cold & soar throat. I can scarsly speak.
Sat 20th	Very ill this day. Taking opening medium and other alterives [alternatives?] to produce sweat.
Sun 21st	I had a fine sweat this morning after 3 o'clock and before 6. I had the bed all over wet. I hope I shall receive benefit by.
Sat 27th	A fresh fall of snow last night. It really has become so deep that the poor birds and game are laid dead in many places.

Week 5

Complaints of sickness of all descriptions have been very prevalent, the Small Pocks, Mesels, Typhis and other diseases, from the thick cold easterly wind which has continued ever since the snow came on, that is a month, all distempers have been flying about. I have a boy has the Small Pocks, a complete sotter (?) all over his body, and the Scarlet Fever is raging in Newton. 2 familys belonging W Coull are all down, one or two yesterday was not expected to live.

Week 6

...the game are dying, the men have caught several Partrages just dying, and many other of the feathered tribes.

Week 7

This is six weeks snow up till this day 18th and realy it becomes serious. I do not know what will be done if it should continue any longer. The snow is just the same as solid ice, there is no getting the turnips even with Whin Hows and other maleable instruments. The cattle cannot break one without cutting with axes.

Week 8

...I had a cart at Newcastle with Butter Ferkins, he got as far back home as Meldon and was oblidged to leave the cart at Mr Wardley and plunge through the snow with the horse as well as he could. He was just exhausted when he arrived home, was oblidged to be put to bed instantly. Such a season I never saw. Fodder is turning scarse and hay dear.

Week 11

We have got the plows to work again after an abstaining of 9 weeks. So very little done before the storm came on, which will make a very throng time. The small pocks have been very severe in this little village. Two hinds and a servant boy been very ill, such a lepard I never saw, completely full all over and very sick and bad, they are not like the small pocks that I used to see. I am doubtful they are a foreign pock that has come from France they are so very large and so very numerous.

Mon 19th Mar The North.d Hounds at Edington this morning. They have had a long rest, ever since Christmas.

[*William mentions heavy snow every day that week.*]

Sat 31st Began sowing oats this morning but oblidged to leave off from snow.

Week 14

The Great Western Steamer. This vessel built at Bristol now lay'd at Black Wall, London, is to proceed this week for America, ...she sets off for New York and is expected to perform the voyage in 15 days only.

Tue 3rd Apr A fine morning. All hands sowing and harrowing in oats.

Sun 8th A disagreeable rainy day. There is no looking out, wind north and sleet.

Week 17

Lord Durham has set off to Upper and Lower Canada to quel the disturbances that has taken place lately by the Americans wishing to be an independent state and have their own Government.

[*There are two further references to Lord Durham and his problems with the British Government.*]

Wed 25th Attending the funeral of Richd Donaldson, blacksmith, of this place who died last Sunday of small pocks.

Sun 29th A snow storm, a constant snow this morning as Winter like as ever.

Tue 22nd May Our rent day. At Mitford. Pd. Thos Tindale 152 for Henry Revely Mitford Esq for Throphill Hall Farm.

Week 22

We have had just such another Springtime as last year. It was 9th June before there was the least appearance of Spring and until this day 3 June we may say it has been much the same as last after 8 weeks storm and not a day but what was snow and frost and the severest nature.

Sat 16th Jun Rain, rain, rain & the Season turns out very unfavourable. Nothing to do.

The "Plough Inn" c.1900 where William attended meetings of the Mitford Association. This stone building was destroyed by fire in the early 1930s but was later rebuilt in brick to a similar design

Week 26

The Grand Coronation day Princess Victoria (only 18 yrs old) Crowned June 28th all public works laid inn, and rejoicing all over England. Cannons and Guns and Alluminations with a general feasting, all poor people. Roast Beef and Plumb Puddings with Ale was just the order of the day.

Mon 6th Aug Rain, rain, rain for ever and ever, the fruits of the Earth will never come to perfection.

[*Similar comments every day that week!*]

Week 33

A meeting at Newcastle of the British Association to be held tomorrow 20 [Aug]. The town of Newcastle is full of strangers, all the Great Men of all Nations is to be there, about 6 Lords, the Duke of Wellington, Duke North.d, Sir John Herschel and all leading Philosophers and Astronomers in all the kingdoms of the Earth beneath to lecture upon different subjects. Russia, Germany, Sweden, France, Italy, Astria [sic] but in fact all places of the Globe of their most scientific and Astronomy. Lodgings are scarsly to be had in any place of the Town, excepting the suburbs and then some difficulty even at any price.

Week 38

The Corn ripens very slowly. The Irish shearers are low, the best prices are 9/- per week with their victuals. We generally think our own countrymen is entitled to 2 shillings more than the foreigners. Be that as it may, I have seen as good Irish shearers as English, and some a great deal better, but Pat does not require such dainties as the English and the Beds we generally lay them as straw, a blanket and a quilt. Pat is happy and comfortable. They sometimes bring a family with them (that is an objection).

Thur 25th Oct Morpeth Fair for Horses and Cattle. Bought 2 oxen, Mr Brewis, Eshot, @ 24 £.

Fri 23rd Nov At Morpeth getting 100 handbills to persecute to Conviction for theft. Lead W Coull and Self from the Thresher Gang 25£ reward.

[There is no other mention of this event.]

Sat 24th A beautiful day. Had the Morpeth Police examining the premises

1839

[*On the inside cover*:] "No. of my Gold Watch is Robt. Cooper No. 8160 London."

"The population of the World at this time 1839 is
730,000,000 Millions
50,000,000 are Protestants
120,000,000 are Christians etc
9,000,000 are Jews
140,000,000 are Mahomitints

Superstition & Bigatries in all sects of Christians

Gods Name be Praised."

Tues 1st Jan — A very frosty cold day. Threshing Oats. Mr Mitford Greyhounds kill'd 4 Hares upon this farm.

Week 2

The greatest high wind ever I remember of seeing in my life time hapened on Monday last 7th inst. It began about midnight and continued throughout the day until about 5 o'clock at night. It unroofed part of the Houses and tore up part Trees from their roots in Newcastle, Sunderland, Durham, Hexham, Carlisle, North and South Shields, York and as far north as the Tweed. The news has been very alarming, several lives lost, but how far it has extended further we have not heard.

Wed 9th — Not at Morpeth [Mart] today, a very hard frost (prepairing manure).

Week 3

[*Accounts of damage in Dublin due to the storm with houses blown down, fires, roads blocked by fallen trees etc.*]

Sat 19th 40 Bolls Barly Mr John Brewis Turks Head Morpeth @10/-

Week 4

A great meeting is to take place at Newcastle respecting the Corn Laws....

Week 5

[Records the meeting in Parliament re Corn Laws and the return of Lord Durham from Canada.]

Week 6

[Expectations of the Queen's Speach (sic) re Corn Laws - disappointed!]

Sat 9th Feb A tolerable fine day. Sir Matt. Hounds at Needless Hall Moor.

Week 7

Lord Durham is to be examined by both Houses of Parliament respecting leaving Canada before his mission was completed. Lord Brougham has brought charges against him of not bringing the Rebbles to a Court Marshal but transported the Criminals to Burmuda, a small island in the West Indies, whereas by law he should have decapitated them upon the Gallows. Everybody thinks that Lord Durham acted the part of a wise & humain man, but Lord B and the Earl of Durham are no friends.

Tues 12th Feb A Great Battle between two pugilists Deaf Burk and Bendigo for 150 aside, Birmingham. *[A full account of the fight is given on the following page.]*

Week 9

The Northumbrian Assises begin on Friday first [*Mar*]. The people look forward with great anxiety respecting this tryal of Mr Bolam who, it is supposed, should have Murdered the poor unfortunate Mr Millie in the Savings Bank Arcade, Newcastle. This Bolam is a native of Harbottle and of decent respectable pairents and enjoy'd a situation of 100 a year as accountant for the Savings Bank. Millie was found in the office on the evening about 10 o'clock his brains knocked out in the most cruel manner and, is supposed, by Bolam.

Week 10 Mar 4 - 10

The Hinds Hiring for Married Servants at Morpeth on Wednesday [6 Mar].
6 Bolls Wheat, 5 Old Bolls Oats, 11 Bolls Barly and 5 Peas new(?) 3£ Deaf Stint, a pig allow'd in Summer, 2 Fothers [Cartloads] Hay for the cow and to be allowed plenty of straw, a poke Potatos. Sett Bondage Wages 9d per day for small work and 1/6 for Harvest, the Bondager to assist in getting in the stacks and to have one shilling a stack for threshing and winnowing, the single man or men that gets ale money was 13 to 14/- per week, very many anxious for cash, then they find no cows. Those that cannot put on a cow, was allow'd 4 to 4/6 per week in place.

Sat 9th Still snow, the frost is very severe. The snow is half up the leg.

Week 11

The weather becomes very serious, every day worse. Today 17 [Mar] it is most awful, a continual drift of snow from the north east. The wet is down through all the lofts, into the very lowest room in the House.

Thur 21st A general meeting at Harnam Low Hall, my Brother's farm. Greyhound coursing. Fine sport.

Week 13

The Season continues very bad. It has the appearance of starving every thing of the face of the Earth.

Week 14

We have just begun to sow the first of the Oats....about 45 years ago my Grandfather was living (he living at the time of the Scottish Rebellion) and I was at School in Morpeth, he used to say that after 10 o'clock in the morning they had to unloose the Oxen from the plow. In april it was so excessively hot that they could not go, and many times they have sunk beneath the pressure of heat.

Wed 3rd Apr Attending the Magistrates as Overseer of the Poor and as Guardian of the New Poor Law.

Week 15 Apr 8 - 14

My Grandfather George Swan lived at Newton Underwood Parish of Mitford in the year 1740 was attempted to be press'd into the ranks of the Scottish Rebbels. He was a man at the time and was holden the plow in a field called Crawla [Crawley] Hill just west of Leightwater House by the roadside, but got clear by saying that he was not an enemy to Charles but that whoever was king he would be subject and the Chief said "Come along men, he is an honest plow boy". Then he remained at the plow and saw their armies pass forward to Morpeth.

Fri 12th A fine day. The best since Oct.

Mon 22nd A Coldside plowing day. Mr Juet (?) who has taken Middle Coldside Farm @ 300.

Week 18

A very sudden and awful Death has befallen our friend Mr Ephraim Dixon, Wine & Spirit Merchant of Newcastle, who married our Niece Elizabeth Coull of Thornton. He took ill on Friday last 26 and Died on Saturday following of Inflamation of the Bowels. A very sudden Death. He was buried on Tuesday at Morpeth much regretted by all his acquaintances. He has left a wife & 2 children, a Boy and Girl, very fine children, he being 40 years of age. Such sudden deaths should put us in mind of making preparation, for we know not how soon it is to be our lot.

Tues 30th [*Acted as bearer at the funeral in Newcastle.*]

Wed 1st May — Morpeth Fair the Hiring for single Servants. Men asking high Wages 15 to 21 £ per year.

Fri 3rd — All hands sowing clover seeds, a beautiful day. I never saw the land better.

Tues 14th — A tremendious frosty morning. Ice to break off the water in the pump trough.

Week 21

[*Disturbances all over the country; Chartist meetings and a Universal Suffrage meeting on the town moor Newcastle.]*

Week 24

Died last Thursday Mrs Jane Milburn at Longhorsley, an old acquaintance of my poor Mother. She lived in this place when I was born, my mother at that time in a very poor state of health. Mrs Milburn nursed me and ever since she always had a claim upon my generosity. Last time I saw her is about 14 months since, she seemed to be fast going to decay but still she knew me and expressed her kindness by kindly squeesing and holding fast my hand and called me her son. She was a fine old woman, of the old school very few indeed is left behind (of such material). Aged 94 yrs.

Sat 22nd — Ellen at Longhorsley at her Aunt's funeral.

Week 27

[*Chartist meetings. A "Great meeting" at Bedlington; the Military called out from Newcastle, one person arrested and taken to "Burgmingham"*.]

Week 28

[*Riots in Birmingham and the Bull Ring*.]

Week 31

The trial of Bolam for the murder of Mr Millie at the Savings Bank at Newcastle terminated on Thursday last after a long and patient investigation by the Judge and Jury and was found guilty of setting fire to the Bank. The Murder was so mysterious a thing that there was a doubt and that doubt was given in favour of the Prisoner and brought in Manslaughter!!! and is to be Transported to a Pineal settlement for the remainder of his life. He told the Judge that transportation was Death to him. There is not a doubt left in the whole community but that he is guilty of the cruel murder and it is a pity that they could not have made away with the Beast in human shape.

Sun 4th Aug To dine at Thornton today and spend the day. Sister Coull is much confined with Rheumatic Pains not able to move from her chair.

Week 33

Agitation all over England and Scotland with respect to those Chartists as they call themselves. The Magistrates have had to be very vigilant and have swore in a great number of Constables, in Morpeth 250, Newcastle 1000 Speachels (Specials?). The Military have been called out to a great many places and a great number of vagabonds have been committed to Jaol and Houses of Correction. It has been seldom ever known the unsettled state of the Country, the Collarys and Trades of all kinds have been forsed out of employment and Busness quite at a stand.

Week 35

Bolam, the Convict, for the Murder of Poor Millie at the Savings Bank Newcastle is set of for the Hulks in London River last week, to be Transported to Van Deamons Land with the first ship that sails to that Colony. He still declares his Inocency but the Public are to a man fully convinced that he is the Murderer and no person else. It is a strange mistery, for a man in his circumstances to commit such a foul deed, a Man possessed of a great deal of Property and likewise a single person, quite beyond penury and want but the Stain on the Man's Character is highnous. Sodomy is believed!!!

Week 37

Miss Cookson of Meldon Park was Married on Thursday last to an officer in the Army, a Major. She is only 19, a gay wedding. 8 Carrages is at Meldon Chapple after the seremony was over they, the Bride and Groom, was to Dine at Benwel her Brother John's. It is said her fortune is 10,000 there is still two more.
The Weather is most distressing, every day Rain. If you have Half a day fair, the next is sure to be wet. Great fears for the Corn crops, bad accounts from the South and likewise from Ireland, the fall of Rain has been more so there than in this part of the Country.

Week 38

Such a Rain last night never was remembered, the Rivers are all overflowed their Banks, the Flood never known so high. My East Haugh is Maslin, Potatoes and Oats, not a vestage is to be seen. All will be destroyed, the Maslin is cut 17 thraves, the Potatoes a capital crop and the Oats a very great crop. Three Ridges cut and all destroyed. The Corn sheaves are floating down and large Trees at this present moment 10 o'clock Sunday morning. The dismal prospect is beyond calculation, such seasons as the past 6 years never was known in the World. It appears like a Judgement upon the Land. It is God's Judgement and we must submit!!!

Mitford castle in ruins 1812. The castle dates from at least the 12th century.

Week 41

Distressing Account last night from Newcastle, Mr Robert Thompson, Butcher, has stopt payment. I had his two sons last night arrainging with the Creditors to meet at Gateshead on Tuesday first. I myself wants for money & stock £536-2-0. I am very doubtful the Acct.s will be bad. He is seriously taken inn with a Mr Proctor, Merchant on Newcastle Quay. It is said 2000. Proctor has hung himself in his Counting House, has left a Widdow and a family. Such are the ups and downs in life, brought on by Extravigence.

Week 42 Oct 14 - 20

A meeting last Tuesday of the Creditors of Mr Robt Thompson at Kenmurs (?) Attorney, Gateshead, took place when it was declared that his friends would garantee 7/= in the pound, 2/= paid now and the remainder 3 months. I for one being the principal creditor refused the offer. I think there must be more Assets than is represented. My Bill is 540, a very serious account. I have been completely Swindled as he promised me on 25th Sept that 200 should be paid into the Joint Stock Bank, when on 5th Oct there had not been one shilling.

Mon 21st Oct — Set of for Newcastle to meet the Creditors of Mr R Thompson and agreed to take 7/= in the Pound.

Week 45

The Weather of late never in living memory of Man was ever seen such a long continuance of Wet since St Swithin's Day which falls in July. We have ever scarsly had a fair day....

Tue 5th Nov — Rain. Just the same as all this last week. Land bottomless, no more Sowing.

Week 46

At Blyth receiving my half years Rents for House property at Crofton.....£8.10.0 Blyth is a very dull place and not much trade to make a bustle excepting the Shiping. There seems to be a good many Ships in the Harbour. Likewise there seems to be a great number of Carpenters imployed about the Dock. Blyth certainly would be a thriving place if Sir Matthew White Ridley would give a little more encouragement and let them longer Leaces to build upon.

Thur 14th Nov — Took 61 sheep to Turnips at Newton Mill, Thos Vint, at 5 £ per Acre.

Fri 15th — There is a Ceasure made at Newton Mill for Arrear Rent 204 £. Poor Vint.

Tues 19th — The Morpeth Harriers at Newton today. Had a fine run and kill'd two Hares.

Week 51

Land is letting just as high as ever and many applications as new beginners. I should think the worst time than the preasent cannot hapen. That small farm at East Coldside 170 Acres is said is let for the Old Rent and Mr Potts had given it up for Abatement, the Rent 230 £.

Fri 20th Dec — Still Rain and Stormy weather, such a season the Oldest man living never saw.

Sun 22nd — Rain and wet. Geo Brewis down from Angerton to Dinner.

Week 52

The Corn is still in a very bad state for Threshing. The Rollers cannot be kept clear from warping. The Millers complain that it furs up the stones and clags part of the floor all over the different things that comes in its way.....

Mon 23rd — Still Rain. Sir Matt White Ridley's Hounds at Bolam. Kill a fox after a very severe run. Too many foxes.

Wed 25th — Christmas Day. Expect 12 to Dine. Roast Beef, Turkey, Pork, Puddings & Pidgeon Pie.

So ends the year 1839 which I am very sorry to say has proved the worst I ever saw.....

1840

Inside page

A Wedding 90 years ago

On the 7th June 1750 was married at Rothbury, Mr William Donkin a considerable Farmer at Tosson to Miss Ellenor Shotton of the same place the entertainments on the occasion were very grand, there was provided no less than 120 quarters of lamb, 40 ditto of veal, 20 ditto mutton, a great quantity of beef, 12 Hams, with a suitable number of Chickens, with 8 half ankers of Brandy made into Punch, 12 doz cyder, a great many gallons of wine, the company 550 Ladies and Gentlemen deverted by 25 Fiddlers & Pipers the evening was spent gloriously.

The Year begins with very bad forebodings, respecting the state of the Country & likewise the very bad weather that has been as still continues likely still, for the appearances of the very unsettled positions of the clowd and the slompy state of the land no person dare look on, the young wheat is such a state as few people ever recollects of everseeing the Oldest Man living never saw such a year for rain as the past, God forbid, that any of us should ever live to see the like again, during the whole of the past year it has always been a rain on the clowds lowering for a fall, particularly since Midsummer it has been continous rain.

3rd Week Jan 13 – 19

The great topic of Conversation is the Queens Wedding which is said to take place about the middle of next month in Feb'y with Prince Albert of Germany of the Gotha Family of very poor extraction, but England is expected to provide his Excellency with a suitable Income as a consort of the Queen of England say 50,000 (Generous England) you pay very dearly for your follies, but then he is a Protestant Prince, tho part of his family are Catholics, we have been in the habits of getting our Kings & Queens from Germany (as much as to say) the pure blood.

Mon 13	Died at this place Thomas Rutherford aged 70 a Cottager under me.
Fri 17	Sir Matt White Ridley, Hounds at Middliton Bridge, a very fine day.
Sat 18	A hard frost, but plowing at afternoon, land is getting dry.
Sun 19	A stormy, blowing sort of day, several showers of rain.

4th Week Jan 20 – 26

Great riots all over England called the Chartists, and the tryals of Frost and others at Newport has ended of all found guilty of high treason and is to be executed, hung on a gallows and after that their heads to be struck of their bodies and quartered for waging war against the Queen of this Relm, there has been since their condemnation disturbances at Sheffold and Birmingham, they have been put a stop to likewise in London, the authorities have been put upon their guards, to be in readyness.

6th Week Feb 3 – 9

Frost's life with two others are saved for transportation they are arrived at Portsmouth and to be sent forward immediately to their destination. The Queens wedding is to take place tomorrow to Prince Albert, there is to be great rejoicings all over the country. I have got a note to attend Morpeth tomorrow, A R Fenwick Esq. Netherton in the chair, which is expected to be attended with all the principals of the neighbourhood, I hope they will all meet with all general satisfaction and no politics introduced to inflame the people to commit any acts of decorum.

Fri 7 Feb A stormy day, Sir Matt Ridleys fox hounds at Rivergreen whin found and a fine run.

7th week Feb 10-16

The Wedding of the Queen with Prince Albert took place according to expectation with great rejoicings. They were married at St James' Chapel at 12 o'clock and after got Breakfast and set off for Windsor at 4 and arrived at the Pallace at 7 and Dined at 8 attended with all their followers. He is much thought of by reports light hair and much like his father, but only he is poor and requires a suitable income of 30,000 a year, and the Queen enjoys a living of 400,000 so much for Royalty, John Bull pays the Piper and happy!!! I should doubt very much if we have not a change of expenses allowed by the Country.

8th week Feb 17 – 23

A great stir at Morpeth to elect a representative to serve in Parliament in place of Lord Liviston who has excepted office as private Secretary in the Home Department, the candidates are the Hon. Howard Son of Earl Carlisle, and Major Hodgin Cadogin of Brenkburn Priory, the contest is carried on with the greatest spirit and neither party will give in, but it is expected Howard is to be the likeliest person to succeed.
The Tories Cadogin, with Mr Mitford, Cookson, Graswell, Lawson and Watson will be beat out of the field, Lord Carlisle's interest is very strong the freemen will likely cline(?) to that side.

9th Week Feb 24 – March 1

The H'ble Howard second son of Earl Carlisle is duly returned from Morpeth in place of Liviston who has taken place as under secretary for the home department, but still Cadogen is not satisfied he begun the canvis on the Monday morning afresh for the next occasion which is expected to take place in three weeks or sooner and Capt. Howard is obliged to stop and continue the same, it will do a great deal of good for Morpeth, it being a very poor place, will cause a deal of money to be spent in the town, besides they the Freemen will be more independent, and will be more better treated than they hitherto have been, they have been totally under the control of the Carlisle family of late.

Mon 24 — A frosty morning. Banking hard stones from the Water at Meldon Bridge for Turnpike.

Sat 29 — Sir Matt White Ridley Fox Hounds at the Morpeth High House. Kill'd one at Mitford, & had a fine Run with one from Penny hill whin till 4 o'clock.

Wed 4 Mar — The Hinds hiring I got one with a cow, 5 Bolls wheat, 5 old Bolls oats, 11 Barly, 5 Peas, 3£ deaf stn. poke potatoes, sett bondager @ 9d & shearing 1/6.

Sun 8 — A fine frosty day had Thos. Brewis of Blyth to dinner.

11th Week March 9 – 15

A great sale of Farm Stock advertised to place on the 24 and 25 March belonging Mr Joseph Bell of Greensfield in the parish of Alnwick who is become a Bankrupt and has assigned all his effects to 3 trustees, he is bailiff to His Grace the Duke of North[ld], it is supposed he will not pay 5/- in the £, he has been a regular take in, has got hold of all who could spair a little money and very many will be ruined by his false pretences such fellows should be transported to Astralia.

Sat 14 — Meeting a gentleman from Southampton Mr Ross at Morpeth, to look over Wood Lands, to report to our Landlord.

13th Week March 23 – 29

We have had Morpeth Horse & cattle Fair on Wednesday last, and a great show of all kinds of Stock. good Horses was in great request both Blood and Draught, few of the former was shown, but a great quantity of the latter good Draught colts & fillies was well sold, from 30 to 35 £ blood few but much inquired for, a great show of stallions for the agriculture Premiums that was to be given that day, Blood Stallion was numerous the Premium given to a horse out of the County of Durham, the Draught to Coquet side a good black stallion.

Mon 30 — A disagreeable kind of wet day nothing can be got forward but Providing Dung Mr Joseph Wilkinson Plowing Day @ Coldside.

Tues 31 — All hands at the Turnpikes repairing both the Donkson Bridge and Turnpike leading to Dike nook [Dyke Neuk].

15th Week April 5-12

The Quarter Sessions at Morpeth on Thursday the 9th Inst. Not much busness only they, the Magistrates and Spencer Trevelyan Esq of Longwitton Hall have appointed me High Constable for the West Division of Morpeth Ward which is a very high troublesome office beside the expence in other Counties they the High Constables have a salary of 35 to 50 £ but hear in this county we cannot get our expences besides getting a great deal of bad blood by returning a successor.

16th Week April 13 – 19

Swore in High Constable on Thursday before Isaac Cookson Esq. in the presence of Edward Spencer Trevelyan Esq. of Longwitton Hall. Sir Matt White Ridley Baronet was running a fox from Coal Laws, down to Newton and earthed found another in Hartburn Banks and made a turn to Thornton back to Meldon Park and got safe into one of the fleurs(?) of I. Cooksons gardens, there is a great numbers of foxes in this part of the country, Sir Matthew does not kill many.

17th Week April 20 – 26

The Grand Steeple Chace at Morpeth came of on Tuesday last at 3 o'clock the only one that ever was run in North.l.d.

Sat 2 May — At Newcastle today enquiring when Mr R Thompson Butcher intends paying Dividend of 7/=.

Mon 11 — Rain, Rain, Rain ever since Thursday. I am afraid of too much. Flitting a tenant to W Fairfoot's Freehold.

Tues 12 — Rain. Shifting a Man & Family to Amble.

Wed 13 — A Rainy Day could not go to Morpeth. The great Flitting Day for cottagers.

21st Week May 18 - 24

At Blyth yesterday 23rd Receiving the Rents from Crofton Property, £8/10/-. Dined at Mr Hiron's (?) Butcher and was on board of a Ship of his going for Antrip with a Steam Ingine and other goods as a general cargo. I was strongly invited to take a Voyage to Brussels and Antwrip but I declined going at this Season.

Wed 27 — About 800 Oxen at Morpeth Market….

23rd Week Jun 1 - 7

....the people now a days eats mostly Animal food formaly they generally got Oat Meal once a day but times are changed.

25th Week Jun 15 - 21

A most daring attempt to Assassinate Queen Victoria last week by a Young Man 18 yrs old on her leaving Clairmont Pallace along with Prince Albert.....

Wed 24 June — A great Meeting at Morpeth to congratulate the Queen of her escape from Assassination.

28th Week Jul 6 - 12

Oxford, who attempted the life of the Queen is under confinement and to be tried, next week, he fains Insanity as a pretext but still it is supposed he belongs to a gang of bad and evil disposed persons called the Orange Club, Tories etc.

Sun 9 Aug — A beautiful fine Morning, intending going up to the Grange Moor to dine with Brother Robert to get ripe Gooseberries.

33rd Week Aug 10 - 16

The Awful Death of Poor Henry Robinson of Needless Hall which happned on Wednesday last about 11 o'clock on his return home from Morpeth Market he had been selling Lambs and had a cart and Horse, and just after passing the new Stone Bridge leading to Abby Mill the Horse took fright and set off in full spead and run against the stone wall, overturned the Cart upon him and was severely crushed that he only lived about one Half Hour, two Doctors attended but he must have been all crushed.

Fri 9 Oct — At Newton Red House at a Jublee given by Mr & Mrs Robson, Dancing till 5.

Thur 22 — A very fine Morning all hands in the stack garth Roping and finishing Stacks.

Sat 24 — Leading Coals for the Winter 4 ~ 8 per Fother from Morpeth Banks & 3/6 from Fontgreen.

45th Week Nov 2 - 8

[*First mention of Foot & Mouth spreading from the South.*]

Mon 9 — 4 more Oxen taken the epidemic disorder and we are given them all drink.

Wed 11 A very dull Market for Cattle on account of this disease, no person dare buy.

48th Week Nov 23 - 29

My Cows have taken this complaint called Marone amongst Cattle, I have 4 is very bad the Milch will have to be destroyed, likewise the Pigs I have about 12 is very bad it will go through all and every anamal about the Place I wish People may keep clear, many people are complaining of bad heads and severe colds I was in hopes that Frosty weather would clear the County of such miserable contageon but it appears in only feeds the complaint and adds a little more fire to the desease. (God grant a change will take place.)

Thur 10 Dec Wedding Day Mr Thomas Blair of Abby Mills to Miss Thompson only Daughter of Mr Robt Thompson Joiner and Innkeeper Mitford it is expected she will make a good Wife.

51st Week dec 14 - 20

The remains of the Emperor of France Napolian Bonaparte who was exiled upon the Island of St Helena and was intered about 20 years ago, is taken up by order of the French, and brought to France for interment, was to take place on Tuesday 15 Inst there is expected to be great doings, there is a great doubt, if they can keep all quiet, for the late minister M. Theirs is a great Jackobine and wishes to revive a spirit of disaffection throughout all France and a great hatred against England.

Fri 25 Had Robt Coull Esq Brother Robt and W. Brewis from Newcastle Christmas Day.

52nd Week Dec 21 - 27

This year terminates much better than has been experienced for 4 years back since Harvest the weather has been generally good and even to this time a mild favourable time only it is very doubtful that it will be healthy. This Epidemic among Cattle, there is something likewise amongst People such as severe colds and pains all over the Body accompanied with a great sickness and a lothing in the stomach much like the Cattle swelled legs and pains all over the Body.

Thur 31 Dec Had our meeting at Mitford for the Association 26 members at 5/- each Dinner and drink.

1841

Frontispiece William Brewis Jan.y 1st 1841

High Constable for the West Division of Morpeth Ward
ending Easter April 8th Sessions 1841

Rain .... I have heard my Old Grandfather Geo Swan say, about 1730 the seasons was quite different, the Oxen & Horses was to be loosed from the Plow at 10 o'clock in the morning all the April months at that time 2 oxen and two Horses always together, a Boy to drive even in Summer they did the same.

Sun 3rd Jan A very fine Winters Day, I dined at Newton Park, the Mr Humbles was to be there but was disapointed. Still this Decease remains amongst Cattle. Brother Robert has 3 or 4 going about slavering at the Mouth, and very bad it goes regularly thro all kinds of Stock not forgetting Pigs etc.

Week 4

.... Our Expedition to China is under the Command of General Elliott, they have taken two small Islands in the great River leading to Pekin the Capital of his Celestial Empire, they the Chinese now sue for Peace but Elliott should have gone direct to Pekin and demanded restitution for past greviances.

Wed 20th Paid Mr Fairfoot's Rent 25 £ for Freehold in this township one Year.

Week 6

Attending the funeral of John Fenwick Esq belonging Brenkheugh, at Morpeth who has left me in trust to his will last Tuesday. There was about 12 Gentlemen attended a very Stormy Day.

Wed 3rd Feb Attending the Magistrates, giving in a list of Rentals for County Rates.

Week 9

..... Still there is great complaints about the Murrain amongst Cattle and Sheep in Scotland the Turnip Sheep is held very bad & particularly in the Frosty Weather when the Turnips were hard and their mouths sore, they all got into poverty.

Week 10

Sir Matthew White Ridley of Blagdon has made the Gentlemen in North.ld. good sport this Winter with his excellent pack of Fox Hounds about 50, Couple of first rate Horses. They have been Killing a great number of Foxes during the Spring months, this last week they have destroyed 8 Old Foxes which is considered very good work but still they are very numerous in this part of North.[ld]. The Lambs in danger.

Wed 3rd Mar — Hinds Hiring at Morpeth. Hired a man & son. Son 8/= per week Hind 5.5.6 . Oats, Peas, Barly 3 £ deaf stint.

Sun 14th — A beautiful Morning. Intending to go to North Middleton to Dine along with Brother Robt.

Sun 28th — A beautiful fine Morning called Carling Sunday. Boiled Peas and Whiskey.

Week 14

Mr Robt. Coull of North Middleton, my Nephew, set off for London on 4th April in the London steamer. He intends visiting many places before he returns, London, Dover, Southampton, Nettlecomb, the seat of Sir John Trevelyan of Wallington, and expects, if found practical, to France, to see the great Capital of Lowis Phillip the now reigning King of France, it is a fine time of the year, the Weather has been remarkably favourable and I hope he will enjoy a great treat, now when such communication of steam.

Sun 4th Apr — Mrs & Anne Brewis from Newcastle Dined here with Geo & Ann from Low Angerton.

Wed 7th — A meeting of the Guardians at the Board Room Morpeth to appoint Chairmen.

Thus 8th — Attending the Quarter Sessions at Morpeth appointing new High Constables.

Week 15

Attending the General Quarter Sessions at Morpeth on the 8th April to deliver up my Office as High Constable of the West Division of Morpeth Ward the collections for my Quarter amounts to £715..14..8d but could not get one farthing allow'd as expences. It seems strange that all Publick offices are paid excepting the High Constable with all their trouble and a serious expence. I return'd Mr Robt Gardner, Low Angerton Land Agent, a very fit and proper person but very unwilling to except Office, we drew a Memorial sign'd by the 4 Const. to the Magistracy but was denied any redress.

Wed 21st — Attending the Board of Guardians, some angery discussions etc.

Sat 12th Jun — At Sunderland Receiving my House Rent 13£.

Above – Morpeth market place 1833

Below - Bees Wing, the famous race horse owned by Mr Orde of Nunnykirk.
She won 51 out of 64 races between 1835 and 1842.

Thur 24th — Morpeth Election great Canvasing Capt Howard and Major Cadogan Brenkburn, as candidates, the place in uproar.

Fri 25th — Bees Wing, Mr Orde's Mare win the Gold Cup yesterday at Newcastle beating the best Horse in the World, called Lanarcost.

Mon 28th — At Newcastle swaring to a Debt of £420.1s due to me from R Thompson Butcher Newcastle.

Fri 2nd Jul — I had 3 Gentlemen waited upon me this morning at 6 o'clock for Lord Osaldson & Baker Cresswell and 11 o'clock 2 for Lord Howick.

Sat 3rd — Electioneering for Lord Howick. Fine Hay Day.

Week 28

[*Very busy with the election. No mention of farming for three weeks!*]

Sat 10th — I voted this morning for Lord Howick as a liberal, the ods are against him in not being prepared in time.

Sun 11th — I here that Howick is 65 short of the Tories, which is a great pity.

Week 29

The Candidates all met at Alnwick on Monday, to Chair* the two members Lord Osaldson & Baker Cresswell who is duly returned Lord Howick made a long speach accusing the two successful members for their double dealing.

*[*William was Chairman for the meeting.]*

Thur 15th — St Swithin a watery Saint, but I would fondly hope & trust is a lie.

Week 31

[*Many scathing comments on the suitability and capabilities of the two successful candidates!!*]

Tue 24th Aug — The New Parliament and the Queens Speach today. Sir Robt Peel takes the Premiership.

Sun 29th — Had Mr Robt Potts Rothbury Geo Brewis & Thos Bell Newcastle at Dinner, a very fine day.

Week 37

Morpeth Races commenced on Wednesday last, good Racing but very few Gentlemen to Patronise the Sport. I fully expected the Tories would have appeared in full force but they have got their turn into Parliament therefore that is all they want. Capt Howard, Member for Morpeth had his Band of Music playing all the time but no Sport from the Tory side. They are affraid they cannot retain their seats should any rupter arrise it will be up with Sir Robt Peel their darling Pet of the Fancy, but time trys all.

Sun 26th Sep — Expect Mrs Murton and Miss Coull to dinner along with Brother Robt & others.

Sun 3rd Oct — A very fine morning but the Rainbow appears in the West. What that sign may be time only can tell, future events only belong to the great power above.

Week 41

[Rain every day.] Rainbow appearing in the west has had a very bad effect.

Week 42

Whatever will be the consequence God only knows but such a succession of heavy Rain never was known by the Oldest Person living….

Week 45

A very great censation has been over all the Country respecting the Burning of the Tower of London, such a conflagration seldom happens in England about 150,000 stand of Arms besides all the great Trophies gain'd in the memorials of Englands Glory over all the World, and real curiosities of all descriptions, the Crown Jewels a scramble for to get them saved, it is estimated 200,000£ will not cover the loss to the Nation, the confusion attended on such occations, caused much more loss than otherwise would have been such a number of all kinds of People, some plundering all the time.

Week 46

News Arrived from London yesterday by the Mail that a Prince was born on Tuesday last 9th and after the news at Morpeth just before I left at 3 o'clock the Guns and Bells were set a Ringing, and that the Mayor had got order to give to the Publick a great quantity of Wine, but I immediately said it would be another Pention upon the Country. Therefore we as subjects had no occation to rejoice for that we would have to subscribe to keep him at this time we have as many as we could manage.

Week 47

A great Meeting on Wednesday next by requsison of the High Sheriff Sir Matt White Ridley, Blagdon to congratulate the Queen & Prince Albert on the Birth of Prince and Heir to the British Throne of these Relems, signed by most of the respectable gentlemen in the County, it is expected Sir Matthew will be honoured by Lord Blagdon when Presenting the Petition in Person, he is a young man just Married to Judge Barron Park's only Daughter it is expected he will get a great Fortune with her, he keeps 50 Couple of Fox Hounds to entertain the Sportsman in Northumberland.

Week 48

The Duke of Northumberland attended the County meeting on Wednesday last to congratulate the Queen & Prince Albert on the Birth of Prince and Heir to the British Throne of these Relems, the Members of the County Lord Osseldson, Baker Cresswell as the present Members, likewise Lord Howick, Earl Grey was expected but sent a note with His Grace the Duke to signify the disappointment he felt on not attending from indisposition. The busness was soon got over, as there was little to say and less to do. Politicks was never mentioned otherwise Lord Howick would have been down upon them.

Week 49

The Rents are mostly over and it appears there will be a great many Farms to let. Gentlemen thinks they ought to have more Money and Farmers thinks they ought to be less.

Thu 2nd Dec A great Greyhound Course for a valuable Cup 150 £ at Bothel Domesne Today.

Week 51

Bad Accounts and great distress of all the Counties in England for want of Trade and upon other things very many of the Banks all over have suspended payments and above all the Berwick Bank just in this immediate neighbourhood, I see by the Gazette that they the Partners Batson, Wilson & Berry are become Bankrups, when that takes place there is seldom much paid, it will do a great deal of harm all about the Tweed when there are little else in circulation, many a man will be ruined.

Week 52

Our Association was held at Mr Robt Thompsons Plow inn Mitford on Thursday last, and 18 Members Dined and spent a very agreeable day, our amount does not exceed 26 Members, we have decreased very much, since the County prosecutes all criminals, which many one think it relieves them from associating to prosecute to conviction, still I think it a very friendly meeting. We had T. Bullock Esq, Benj. Bullock Esq, Benj. Thompson Esq, Robt Coull Esq, J. Robson Esq and many other respectable Gentlemen.

1842

Another eventful Year has just closed on a portion of our Political existance and are on the threshold of its successor, which portends many events of exceeding magnitude. It is very gratifying to contemplate that is to come and success may attend Great Britain for the Year 1842 but disgrace and mortification, and the canker of remorse has attended all our actions of late, the Sircen (Saracen?) and the China Wars is a blot England cannot yet clear off. The Thousands that have been slain wantonly and likely to be so, for avarice and bigotry, superstition and the love of conquests that the English are so fond of.

Wed 5th Jan A full Market of Stock and the Prices a shade lower. The Failure of the Berwick Bank has caused a greater influx.

Sun 8th A tremendious Frost, the Turnips Sheep & Beasts cannot break them, we have this day, have recourse to axes as a substitute to slice them.

Week 3

The Account from China is better, our Troops are getting forward upon the eastren shores of the great Empire have taking Canton, Custen, Amoy and Nankeen, these are strong holds on the eastren side. They are intending from the last accounts to lay up for the Winter before they attempt Pekin, the Capital. The Chinese have made little resistance to our Troops. Amoy is a very strong place Battries laid with Granite stone cased over with Clay and mud but they landed the Soldiers both sides of the Ramparts, the Inhabitants flew in all directions & the British had not a Man slayed.

Week 4

Complaints all over the Country, of great distress particularly amongst the Manufactories, in some places particularly Manchester, Wakefield, Leeds & Hudersfield the poor are half starved for want of work and the complaint of the restriction upon the importation of Corn, and other things of use, the distress is beyond precedent. Soup kitchens are all over the Country and subscriptions of all kinds to find the people in work, they the inhabitants and neighbours around Morpeth have raised 100 £ and given the workmen 15d a day upon the Common as improvement.

Week 5

The Christening of the Young Prince on Tuesday 25th Inst to be called Albert Edward Prince of Wails, and a great may more in succession. The King of Prusia is arrived to be Godfather with others great doings is expected at Winsor, Dinner at 5 o'clock and to be attended by all the Ministers of State, likewise all the Bishops who always have to be at the head when any good things is to be given away. I suppose we will have to be saddled with other 50,000 a year to be pinched out of John Bull. Johnny has much to bear but he must take it quietly whether he is able or not.

Tues 25th Snow. A complete Drift all the Road fill'd. 8 Men Casting Snow upon the Turnpike.

Week 7

Parliament has met for the dispatch of busness with Sir Robert Peel at the head the first thing is the changes in the Corn Laws….
…but the Aristocricy are anxious to keep prices high, to keep the Rents of Land up, but Distress crys aloud for Bread.

Week 8

We had Sir Matt Ridley's Hounds threw off at this Place, yesterday 19th [Feb] a very beautiful firm morning but then it was 11 before they sett of. Sir Matthew was very pleasant, he complemented me in having such a pleasent residence, he thinks Throphill the beautifullst place in this part of North.ld. for a Seat House just upon our hill or upon the son all (?) Freehold on the east side. His Father admired the situation, being between the two rivers, and such a beautiful Vale down the Wansbeck to Morpeth (it certainly would be).

Mon 28th Apr Easter Monday. Attending Mitford Church as Churchwarden.

Week 14

Petitions all over England against Sir Robt Peels measures, he has taking such a large survey of the different articules that pay little or no duty at this time. The Property & Income Tax makes people stumble both Trade & Farmers more so the Agriculturist, there is no appeal 300 a year Rent pays 150 Income without the chance of Appeal…

Week 16

The Meeting at Morpeth on Wednesday last was well attended. The High Sheriff Riddle of Cheesebourngrange opened out the Meeting with a short speech which was followed by Mr Donkin, Bywell ….
…all condemn the principals of Sir Robt Peel particularly the Income Tax a dangerous impost in time of Peace.

Week 19

Morpeth Fair was well attended on Wednesday last [4th May] both by Masters and Servants. Men was plentiful at 5 to 9 £ for the Half Year and very many left unhired but Woman are generally wanted at the Whitsuntide their wages 3 to 5 £ for the Half Year, and rather scarse.

Fri 13th May A beautiful fine day. The great Flitting Day for Cottagers, very throng.

Mon 16th Mrs Heron of Blyth, Mrs Brewis Hartlepool and Brother Robt here today.

Week 21

The prisoner Good who murdered the woman in Surrey near London and cut her into pieces and burnt most part of her Body, in the Stable, was hung on Monday in London, the number of people is supposed to exceed 100,000.

Week 23

The State of the Country is such that all Trades are at a stand it is pitiable to see the number of unimploy'd labourers of work, the new Ministry has made a sad change since they came into office, what with the Income Tax and the new Tarriff, as it is called. Trades people scarsely know what to do, it has had a very serious effect on all situations of people, both Gentlemen, Farmers, and Traders, all say they do not know what is to be the event but it is generally supposed it will turn out for the worse.

Tues 31st Jun Mrs Murton looking at a house at Mitford to dwell in.

Week 25

A severe Drought. Everything is quite burnt up….

Week 27

Mr Orde of Nunnikirk has refused, for the noted Old Mare Bees Wing, 6,000 Guineas but the reply to them was, she was the property of the People of Northumberland that he could not part with such a valuable treasure without risking their displeasure. When she won the Gold Vase at Ascot, the Queen of England solicited Mr Orde to know the value of such a treasure but his answer was the same, she was the Property of his native hills the County of Northumberland and that money was no object. (An Old Batcholor!!)

Week 28

The Queen's life has again been attempted the 3rd time with a Pistol by Idle and ignorant Youths……..Oxford the first, next Frances the second and last I forget his name, is the Son of a Journeyman Brazier a youth of about 17 descripted and a hunch on the back, the first confined for life, the second is Transported & I hope this will be hanged.

Week 29

Died on Wednesday last [13th July] our Friend and our Cousin Ralph Carnaby Esq of Shawdon Wood House a very stout and gross made man I should say nearly 20

Stones but a real worthy character. A man I should say, never did Ill to no person, but a good natured peaceable person long Steward for the Hargreaves family of Shawdon, and I should say by them much regrated, he has left only Brother John who was Attorney some time in Morpeth, their Neice was kill'd by Thunder in the House at Shawdon by the electored fluid entering the chimney.

Week 30

R Carnaby Esq formerly lived at Todburn who was born then his father James Carnaby Married my Mothers younger Sister they farm'd Todburn and Hedley Wood & the west Field near Rothbury before they left for Shawdon where my Aunt Mrs Donkin Miss Donkin Daughter of the above who was kill'd by Thunder in the House and the late Ralph, the only surviving of the family is John, a very quiet and an inoffensive man but not brought up to Farming, consequently he will leave the place on May first and retire to some quiet place to spend the remainder of his days.

Week 35

The Harvest is in its greatest throng, the weather continues very favourable, the Harvest work will soon be over if the weather continues favourable. I have about 26 Hands at work……this will prove the best season since 1826.

Week 36

The Queen of England and Her Husband Prince Albert has gone down to Edinborough and a Visit to her Scottish dominions, by Sea, in a Steamer called the Royal George, accompanied by two or three more. She has been sea sick, and it is said she intends to return by Land, so that we expect to see her pass Morpeth. She has been well received in Old Reaky but her Minister Sir Robt Peel, the popolices have pelted him with stones and rotton Fruit. He could not expect much better.

Sun 18th Sep At Newton Park to Tea with Brother James, a very warm day.

Week 39

Mr Orde's Bay Mare Bees Wing has won the Doncaster cup this year again. The People in Newcastle have, it is said, won Thousands she has beaten all the Don's and win in a common Canter!! 3.000 £

Fri 30th Meeting the Barristers at Morpeth Court to revise the list of Voters for County Members. 3 Voters in this Township, Brewis William, Fairfoot Edward & Moor Willm, these are the Voters acknoledged.

Week 43

The Funeral of Mr Orde was yesterday at 1 o'clock at Morpeth Church the place where his friends lay, there was a good number of People Voluntureły went along with a number of Gentlemens Carrages, 2 Mourning Coaches and about 8 Carrages and 80 Pedestrians. He Died much respected although a little Penicous in habit yet a true friend to the Poor, his gait was odd, very seldom a good Hat, and very often a thread bare coat, his Man Jack and he in a Gig, often quarreled about shewing respect, and Mr Orde has often offered John his Hat if he thought it better than his own.

Week 45

Morpeth Bridge Toll. Money in hand arising from 5 Oct last is 4683-12-0 I hold two shares 200-0-0 at 5 per cent is 10-0-0 now the Property Tax is to be paid out @ 7d per £. It is a pity that they the Trustees should not pay the one half off, and reduce the Toll, it would do a great deal to the Township of Morpeth, but like all Publick busnesses it is kept back to pay hangers on such as Clarks etc etc they pay 5 per cent to us and receives 3 from Government securities.

Week 47

......Beggars are never from the Door, it is distressing to see the great objects that are constantly in the streets and lanes scarsly Stockings or Shoes (on) their Feet, and nothing upon the back to keep the Could out.

Week 48

A Peace made with China after taking a great number of their seaports Canton, Cushin, Nankin and several others with a sum of 21 Million of Dollars payable in three years....

Week 52

A great deal of Murders and Thefts are committed in all parts of the Country...but what can be expected when Trade in all its branches is newly at a standstill and Poaching for Game has likewise become a very great evil...

Sun 25th Dec A fine morning expect Brother Robt and Geo Brewis from Angerton.

.....If the present Ministry cannot devise some other plans to relieve the Country, I am affraid it will turn to desperation. Men will lose Heart and do acts of Violence, the People of England have been looking forward these few years past for a change for the better but every change they have been disapointed.
Oh, England!!!

Remains of the ruined 14th century Manor House, Mitford.
above – postcard c.1910 below – 1812 engraving

1843

The New Year commences with festivities and disorder, there is no public place to resort, that we do not witness an emmence moral advance with respect to the working classes, and it is singular that the greatest improvement is to be found when the Clergy has had the least influance. Christmas has exhibited the beneficial influance of opning to our Poor our national Institutions to the working classes on the Sunday, the day on which alone the Poor can enjoy themselves never was a time the Poor stood so much need of success as at this time, Hundreds are traversing the Country seeking work, but cannot get any thing to do, few people have anything to spare and every one has enough to provide for themselves.

Week 2

People are looking forward this New Year for the meeting of Parliament to relieve the distress of the Country, all Trades are anxious for some improvement in expectation that times are at the worst. Sir Robt Peel the Prime Minister and the Parliament must endeavour to satisfy the Trades and poor People for a more regular trade so that People can get Bread by the sweet of the Brough, now at this time there are few hands employ'd, only those who have Friends, or good workmen has a chance.

Week 4

A great meeting at Newcastle of the anty Corn Law League and a W Cobdon held forth that a free trade upon Corn would benefit all classes... There must be something done to relieve the Poor labourer for the one Half the Country are next to starving, the capital has disapeared out of the Land altogether and the People are all dissatisfied with our Rulers, causing nothing but begging and starvation. I hope things will take a turn?

Week 5

Such a beautiful Season has never happened in my recollection Since last year May, we have had a continuance of mostly dry weather, now at this time when I am writing there are some people talking of their Springs being so very low that the Wells will not support the House use, the small Riverets scarsely make a run, how strange it makes appear, particularly those five years past, to have such a continuance of wet weather and then at this time complaining in the middle of Winter to want rain.

Sun 29th Jan	Mr W Coull, Geo Brewis & James here today to tea at afternoon.
Monday 30th	Paid Mr Robson Income & Property Tax for farm, Landlord £9..12..5 Tenents £4..6..0

Wed 1st Feb — A cold day. Sir Matt Ridley's Fox hounds at Edington run a fox past this place to Morpeth.

Thurs 2nd — Threshing Oats. The Meeting of Parliament, Sir Robt. Peel will stand with a hot face.

Week 7

Bad Times, this Tariff of our Minister has had a most serious change upon all Trades, and every one is complaining, all Busnesses is at a stand still, the Shipping interest is as bad as all others, Ships to be sold and all agreements of joint stock are done away with, and the companies property sold off, Ships at about 3,000 is not worth 1500, all articles that a Farmer deals in is just one third less, Corn, Cattle, Sheep, Butter & Eggs, all alike cheap.

Mon 13th — A cold north wind, had a plow at Stanton Mill giving a days Plowing to a entering Tenent.

Week 10

Sir Robt Peels finance is falling a great deal short of his expectation this last year of his Administration he is short of his expectation three Millions now the Property & Income Tax he calculated to raise 3,500,000 has raised I suppose nearly 7,000,000 which is considerably more than his calculation that shows he is a very bad Financer and the Country is in great distress, all trades are quite at a stand, all in Poverty.

Thurs 2nd Mar — Delivering 72 Bolls Wheat to Mr Blair of Abby Mills @ 11/-, bad price.

Week 13

The Distress of the Country still continues and one Half the Population is without the means to supply their Family with the Nicessaries of Food and raiment the plaices of refuge, Poor & Workhouses are cram'd to an overflow, the Poor Rates are all advanced. Sunderland is now at 18/= in the Pound Rent. We ourselves are doubled the last year I have paid into the Union nearly 60 £ which is considerably more than has been charged in late Years.

Mon 20th — Dull and very foggy. Sir Matt Ridleys Fox Hounds at Meldon Park but did not throw off.

Sat 25th — Sir Matt Ridleys Fox Hounds met here ½ past ten. Went to Nunriding & found a fox.

Week 16

A meeting was held at the County Courts Morpeth on Wednesday last 12th, to Petition against the Income Tax which was mostly held by Farmers, a very large concourse of people attended by the High Sheriff….

Week 18

The Duke of Sussex Died last week after a short illness much lamented by all classes, a real good Man, Liberal to all institutions was the best of the Royal Family, left a second wife the Duchess of, or Lady Underwood likewise the Queen has been safly delivered of a fine Princes, this makes the third which is very quick for the time married, she is a strong little Weoman, and gets thro without much sickness, a Boy & two Daughters going charmingly.

Wed 26th Apr — An arbitration of some property at Lonsdale Cottage by Mr John Moor, High House and myself for Trustees of the Road & W Robson.

Week 20

Government has proposed an Educational Plan for the Teaching of Factory Children, and the Poorer Peoples Children, but then on a National Plan so that the Disenters are debarred of being teached after their own creed, that the Schools are to be Taught nothing but by the Clergy and Bishops plans and the Church lethurgy in all the Schools, consequently they the Whigs are set up against and Petitions are sent all over England, Scottland and Ireland against the Plan of National Education.

Thur 11th May — A beautiful fine day. Washed the Hoggs to clip in the Wansbeck river yesterday.

Sat 13th — The Hinds Flitting Day, a Drizzly day of Rain.

Sun 14th — A very fine morning, Turning out the Cattle to Grass after Turnips.

Week 22

Great disturbances in Ireland likewise in some of the large Manufactories, the People cannot be kept quiet for want of work… Sir Robt Peel has made sad havock in all busnesses no one has escaped getting a share of the bad prices….

Fri 26th — Paid Mr Tindale Half a Yrs Rent due Martinmas last for Henry Revely Mitford 152 £ yesterday.

Week 23

Such a disagreeable season never was seen in this part of the Country by the oldest person, I cannot recollect since we had a fair day. It is doubtful about the growing crops of Corn and Grass, the Servants are just laying about the place doing nothing, we neither can get on the Land or Hedges or can even stand out to do nothing. How the Turnips will be got inn it remains a mistery…

Fri 9th Jun — Rain. Tremendious weather, most like Noahs Flood, never fair.

Tue 4th Jul — Stagshawbank Fair a beautiful fine dry morning, Turnips want rain.

Week 28

Great disturbances in Ireland. O'Connell and his party are collected 50,000 strong suing for what they call the Charter…

Sat 15th — St Swithins Day all fair, a fine Hay day and no rain.

Sun 16th — A dry morning a Shower of Rain would do good, particularly Turnips.

Sat 19th — A tremendious hot day. West India weather, there is no bairing the sun.

Sun 20th — Rain at 12 o'clock but fair towards the evening. Had Mr Coull & Geo Brewis to tea at afternoon.

Thur 24th — Winning Stones at Rivergreen Mill for the Highways.

Fri 25th — Leading hard stones from the River with 3 Carts and 5 Men.

Week 36

Another meeting is called in east & west Glendale Ward to Memorialise the Magistrates for a reduction in the Sallaries of the Public Services of the Clerk of the Peace, Bridge Surveyor and the Clerks at the private Sessions in consequence of the Rate Payers comming forward to Petition the Justices will be forced to listen to the complaints of the People, what a shame they will force upon the People exorbitant Sallarys for the mere fancy of the Aristocracy Jurisdiction.

Sat 9th Sep — A bright sun suffocating hot, the Shearers are quite knocked up.

Sun 17th — A fine bright morning, I never remember such a beautiful Harvest Weather so far. Thank God!!!

Week 40

All finished up with the Harvesting, and the best I ever remember of ever seeing all the time not a lost hour. The Corn is all got 'so far' excellently good, but the Gift as is called is bad it will require from 3 to 4 Stooks a Boll, which is very bad increase, but the Straw is beautiful white and the Oats threshed a beautiful but in general light Crop upon the ground.

Sun 15th Oct — Mr Tindall, Geo, Richard, James, Bob, Hannah and Mrs Shakerly here on a visit to Tea.

Week 43

The seed time is much like the Harvest, for the Land is so dry and looks so well, and so very clean of weeds, that it is like a garden, we are all well pleased with our station in respect of the seasons if the Country was only well governed, but our laws are badly framed and the expences of the Government so very extravigant the Corn laws are bad and this last Tarriff laid on by Sir Robert Peel has destroyed all confidence.

Sun 22nd — A fine fresh Morning. Brother James is here stopping.

Sat 18th Nov — Sir Matt Ridleys Hounds here today. Kill'd at Leightwater House.

Week 49

The Cattle Bought for Wintering has got that bad distemper called the Moreign, I have 2 just taken it, it is a sad complaint, it reduces the Cattle to mere skeletons…

Week 51

Mr Cookson of Meldon Park has made a claim of some land situated on the Boundaries of our Landlords possession in one place in the west haugh adjoining the River, containing about 10 perches of Sand and Gravil, and in another place called Whittle hill Bridge, a corner taken off the Road which I took and fenced inn about 14 years ago, I think in March 1829 called the Muggers rest, but before Mr C when the Greenwich Hospital there was never a claim.

Week 52

It is most astonishing that such a beautiful fine Weather at this season of the year. Christmas day just like Spring or Summer…

The Old Year wears away and has been the finest Autumn, the oldest person living never saw such a nother, we have scarsely ever had a shower of Rain since the great fall in May & June…

The Old Year is finished there has nothing occurred particularly to mark its memory…

1845

Week 2

I had the Hounds of Sir Matt White Ridley here on Saturday 4th, a little frosty, Sir Matthew sent his Servant early on the Morning to say that it would be 11 before the Hounds would throw off, consequently I had a Number of the Gentlemen took a little Brandy and Whisky with a little cake and chatted away about the favourable Season, and the state of the Country, they threw off at Nunriding Broad Wood and found two…

Week 3

Died much respected Robert Bullock Esq on yesterday Sunday at 4 o'clock at afternoon aged 84 years at Spittle Hill, Nephew to the late W Bullock Esq of the same place who died about 40 years ago, a great Sportsman who kept a Pack of Fox Hounds, supposed to be the best in England. My Father joined him and kept a couple of the said Hounds, they at that time run Badgers upon Meldon Park hills that place was all in grass and was kept as a Park for Dear belonging to Meg of Meldon.

Week 5

We have had our Meeting of the Mitford Association on Thursday last, 21 Members, we expend 5/= each Member, and scarsely exceed 8 or 9/= to cover all expenses, which is very moderate, we have lost our old Member R Bullock Esq, a worthy old man, likewise his two sons Benjn. & Robert, who both Died an untimely death from Spirits and other impropriety's, now Spittle Hill and Newton Underwood has got into the Hands of the Thompsons and the line of the good old Englishmen is gone, and the old Addage of seldom comes the better!!! but trial will prove all.

Week 6

Parliament has met on the 4th & Sir Robt Peel, the Minister, will have to open out the ways & means to be pursued for the Country… They should cut off all useless places and restrain the expences of Royalty!!!

Mon 10th Feb — Paid Mr Mitchel Nunriding, Half years Property Tax for Throphill Farm £6..11..11

Tues 4th Mar — A tremendious great discharge of Cannon, to be heard this Morning, 'report', Miss Burdon, Felton, Married, a fat Bullock to be Roasted whole at Felton. Hind Hiring a great number but a slow trade.

Above – The 12th century church of St.Mary Magdalene, Mitford c.1905.

Below – Mitford church 1812. In 1705 a fire destroyed the roof of the nave but services continued to be held in the choir area until it was fully restored in the late 19th century.

Week 12

I attended at Blyth to meet a Mason to take estimate for Building a Stable to a House I have at Crofton, the expense to finish a new Stable with two Stalls is to be 20 £ for Stalls setting walling Paiving etc. I have let the same to Mr William Cowans Butcher for the annual Rental of 12.10 he to be at the expense of cleaning sweeping all the cobwebs of 'there being many'. It was occupied for 15 years by Forster & Thos Lonsdale, and the Rooms has never been done nothing since they first entered. I hope I have a better Tenent will clean all the filth away.

Sun 16th — At Hartburn Grange Moor paying a visit to Brother Thos. who is poorly.

Mon 24th — Easter Monday, at Mitford Church, a meeting of the Four & Twenty.

Wed 14th May — Paid tithe for Fairfoot's Property, W Lawson 17.3 for one year

Week 22

Mr Hudson has got the line of Railway between Newcastle and Berwick as a Locomotive apparatis. Lord Howick tried for an Atmospherick line, but not being tryed in England the Bord of Trade gave it in favour of Hudsons line, as the other has never been tryed in these parts, but it is believed the compressed air will be adopted as being more safe and better calculated for speed, in Ireland it is fairly tested and answers well.

Week 24

Died at Hartburn on Thursday morning after a protracted illness, the Vicar John Hodgson the Reverend who wrote the History of Northumberland and since he has enjoyed the living at Hartburn has caused a great deal of anamosity in the Parish from extracting all manner of tithes….that never was paid before and the foolish parish gave inn, was affraid to try at Law, now poor man he has gone before the greatest Judge, when all hearts are laid open, to give an account of our past works.

Fri 18th Jul — Cash received of Mr Brumell Solicitor Morpeth as part payment on the Toll secured on Morpeth Bridge 50 £.

Fri 25th — Paid W Mitchell Nunriding Half years Property Tax for Landlord & Tenent
£ 6..4..7 ½ d

Thu 31st — Thunder & Rain has 8 Masons Building a New Cottage & Hovel.

Fri 1st Aug	Misses Hawdons & Miss Wilson from Morpeth Dining here today.

Wed 6th	A meeting in Morpeth to endeavour to establish a Cattle Market as heretofore.

Sat 9th	Leading Stones from the River for the new hovel we are Building.

Week 35

Parliament is all broke up, and the Members are all scampering of to the Moors Shooting, and other sports, while the Queen & Prince Albert are of to Germany to see their Friends at Coburg and Gotha, to see whether there is any more knowledge, as the place has ever been Proverbial for silly people, they have had great doings, every Sunday, Dancing & Music, Balls and Plays with a succession of discordant Music!!!

Wed 3rd Sep	The first opning out of Morpeth Market after the change at Newcastle.

Week 39

A most serious accident befell Mr Robt Coull of South Middleton in Friday last, being out with the Shearers cutting Oats, having the double barrel Gun and Pointer with him, standing resting with his right hand upon the Gun mussel believes the Pointer passed between him and the Gun, caused the cock to strike the cap or fuse and exploded, went straight through the middle of his hand, the same as a Bullet and made a round hole a finger would go through. I was seeing him last night he appears to find great pain.

Wed 1st Oct	Bought 30 lambs for Brother Robert at Morpeth @ 16/- . Sold 30 Bolls of wheat @ 15/- .

Tue 21st	All hands leading Oats, my Brother Robt sent 2 carts & 3 men.

Thu 30th	Attending my Landlord [*Mr Mitford*] at W Brummell Office to give evidence of the Common at Newton.

Week 45

After the Moraine amongst the Cattle next comes the decease amongst the Potatoes. It is doubtful whether there will be any that will keep for seed over Winter…

Sat 8th Nov	Taking up potatoes. We find them mostly all deceased & unfit for use.

Week 46

We have our Quittance at May next…

Wed 3rd Dec	Had an offer for the Farm at W Appleby's valuation but refused to comply.
Fri 5th	Mr Dryden here from Morpeth. Paid him for 4 Gall Whisky £ 2..15..0
Thu 11th	Taking the farm this day for one year 400 £.

Week 50

...I have agreed to give 400 £ yearly for one year to see what will happen after the Free Trade comes into opperation which there is no doubt it will take place. The Ministers have resigned & it is said Lord Russell is called from Scotland to form another administration..

Fri 12th	A cold and stormy day, at Newton Park, Brother Robt but poorly.
Wed 31st	Newton Park Farm Proposals are to be delivered this day. Brother Robert has been defeated by James Scott now on Newton Underwood.

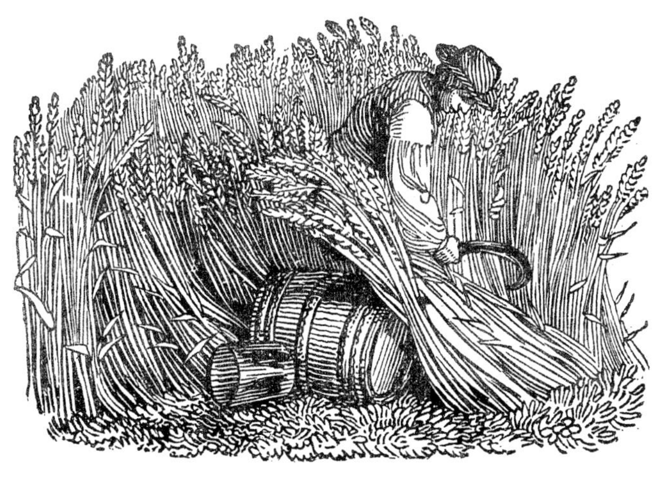

1846

We have had a valuation of our farm by Mr John Appleby Johnston of East Field near Warkworth, we have all taking again at high rents. Newton Park was in the papers two weeks to be lett by Proposals, there was 273£ a year bid by Mr James Scott, Newton but when it came to be pressed to take, he threw up, it then came to brother Robt who has taken it at 235 for liberty for only one year should times keep up.

1st Week Jan 1-4

The farms hang on hard Sir Charles Monk and the Dean of Kirkley have each several places to lett, but they are Gentleman few likes to go near. The prospect is bad, now when full trade in Corn is likely to take place, it will be known as soon as Parliament assembles which will take place on the 22 of this month, there has been meetings all over the principal towns, and the Queen has been memoralised by great numbers.

Thur 1	The first day of the New Year 1846 which begins very favourably in respect of the season, which has come in with fine weather.
Fri 2	Favourable weather for the season of the year fresh and the plows are all going, it has been no stop since Harvest.
Sat 3	We had a wedding at this vilage this day a Mr John Blacket of Long Witton and Mary Watson who lives in this place.
Sun 4	A beautiful fine Winters day, the weather of late has been very favourable for farm purposes.

2nd Week Jan 5 – 11

The Royal Mail leaves London at 9 o'clock nights and proceeds twelve hours between London and Newcastle, how quick, I have known two days. The large steamer leaves Liverpool and arrives in New York in 12 or 14 days, what a quick passage looking at the distance. It is most astonishing what an improvement in machinery within a few years.

Mon 5	Fine plowing weather the season is remarkable favourable.
Tue 6	Still continues fine for the season I hope will continue.
Wed 7	A great wedding today at Melton Park Mr Hardy, Whalton, to Miss Cairons of Melton Park a great many carriages and gigs, set of for Carlisle.
Fri 9	A beautiful day delivering 60 bolls oats at Coxlodge Colliery.
Sat 10	A very fine day all hands plowing for oats, very dry for the season .
Sun 11	A fine morning Mr Brunton sent his mare to grass yesterday.

3rd Week Jan 12 – 18

The country seems in a strange state, in respect of the Corn Laws, petitions are moving from all places, and memorials to the Queen from all the great cities, begging that her most gracious majesty would take it into her Majesty's consideration to allow Grain to be shipped into England, Duty Free, and that it is a cruelty that the staf of life should be kept from the people, when the prospects are so bad, with the failure of the potato crop, which the Irish people most lives upon (then the Landed Proprietors grumble)

Mon 12	Mitford Association held this day at Mitford 19 members dinners @ 5/- each.
Tue 13	A very fine frosty morning, but towards noon a slight fresh
Wed 14	Sold 27 bolls wheat T. Appleby Newton mill at 13/-
Thur 15	Threshing oat, still fresh weather.
Fri 16	All hands at the plows the lea is stif and plows badly.
Sat 17	Plowing land dry and hard.
Sun 18	A wet morning rain most of the day.

4th Week Jan 19 – 25

Parliament has opened out on Thursday 22 the Queens speach from the throne is nothing but a tissue of nonsense as hitherto, the great question of the Corn Laws was never mentioned, Sir Robert Peel has kept that away, not knowing how to deal with it, it is a knotty question and not to be play'd with. Petitions have gone through all the different influential places of any note begging that we may a free importation of Corn from all places, duty free, how it will work in England remains to be seen.

Mon 19	Rain and a cold wind from the south east.
Tue 20	Sold a cow and calf to Matt Robson, Whalton for Newcastle @ 16£.
Wed 21	A fine morning after yesterdays rain Mr Watsons fox hounds @ Whalton.
Thur 22	Threshing a stack of barly, Rain and very soft weather.
Fri 23	A fine morning but the land is very wet plowing for oats.
Sat 24	A fine fresh day threshing oats.
Sun 25	Been Rain through the night but fine at this time 8 o'clock

5th Week Jan 26 – Feb 1

Sir Robert Peel has brought forward his measures for free trade in grain, and the farmers are all up at the prospect thinking that it will bring down the prices to a very low scale, that the foreigners will powr into our country such abundance of grain will render the prices at a ruinous price, but however it will be tried and how it may answer time will determine.
They try all things but never hit on the one that is likely to answer.

Mon 26	A beautiful fine day for the Season, just like a Spring morning.
Tue 27	Plowing for Turnips still continues fresh without snow
Wed 28	Sold 150 bolls barley @ 21/6 to Mr John Brewis, Brewer, Morpeth.
Thur 29	All hands plowing fresh weather.
Fri 30	Sold Mr Brunton Butcher Morpeth 21 ewes @ 23/-
Sat 31	A gloomy day still keeps fresh.
Sun 1	A tolerable fine day still continues fresh.

6th Week Feb 2 – Feb 8

Great stagnation in trade on account of free trade in corn & other provisions. Sir Robert Peel's tarriff has a sweeping measure all kinds of goods is allowed duty free at least a very small duty, he has been a great manefactor of cotton, I should think will be lost in the Corn Laws. We are looking forward for very bad prices towards next year after the new crop comes of the ground there being a failure all over the Continent excepting America.

Mon 2	A fine morning plowing for Turnips the land works well.
Tue 3	Mr Watson's Fox Hounds at Morpeth High House, killed at Molesdon
Wed 4	A cold stormy day, but still not to say bad, still open and fair.
Thur 5	Bought 5 prize pigs of W Cowney Morpeth @ 21/- yesterday at market.
Fri 6	Delivered 60 bolls oats to Coxlodge Colliery to Mr Joseph Hindmarsh
Sat 7	A stormy, windy, cold morning, has the appearance of a storm.
Sun 8	A fine frosty morning, and the weather glass is looking up.

7th Week Feb 9 – 15

It is fully expected Sir Robert Peel will carry all his measures, particularly in the House of Commons, both the free admission of corn duty free and likewise his Tarriffs upon a number of other things. It is passing strange what will be the result, the corn farmer must look to himself, Prices must come down and land in proportion to prices, The landed proprietor will suffer, but not in proportion to the Agricultrest who will be the real sufferer.

M 9	A stormy day, all hands threshing barly for Mr John Brewis Brewer Morpeth.
Tu 10	22/- paid Mr Mitchel Nunriding property tax Landlords £4 –8 –8 Fairfoot – 7 6½ Tenent 2 2 7½
W 11	A frosty morning, all hands leading Dung from the fold yards.
Th 12	A fine frosty day threshing oats to go to Coxlodge Colliery.

Fri 13 — A beautiful fine day, the stakes 5 guineas each by greyhounds at Saltwick or Ogle.
Sat 14 — Delivering 60 bolls common oats Coxlodge Colliery, to Mr Hindmarsh
Sun 15 — A fine morning it has been a remarkable favourable winter.

8th Week Feb 16 – 22

Nothing goes forward but free trade in Corn, Sir Robt Peel proses to make it slide off from all duty in 3 year's time, but it seems the free traders will listen to nothing but a total clear free trade and no restriction. The farmers are holding back for taking land that is advertised in the newspapers at this time, Sr. Charles Monk, the Dean of Ogle likewise have had farms in all winter, but as yet, they have no enquiries after land, and it is a pity they should, as they are both Turks.

Mon 16 — A beautiful fine day, threshing wheat very bad gift.
Tue 17 — All hands plowing wheat stubble for oats, beautiful dry.
Wed 18 — Mr Watson's fox hounds at Newton Underwood, a fine day, wind north.
Thur 19 — Still continues very favourable winter weather and the plowing is forward.
Fri 20 — Mr Watson's fox hounds at Rivergreen, 2 foxes, but very bad sport.
Sat 21 — Delivering 60 bolls of barly to Mr John Brewis, brewer Morpeth @ 21/6.
Sun 22 — A female child born in the village this morning, a daughter of Michael Watson.

9th Week Feb 23 – Mar 1

Great debates in both Houses of Parliament respecting this free trade in Corn. It is expected Sir Robert Peel will have a great majority in the Commons but in the Lords will find great opposition, it will make a great change to the Farmers of lowering the price of Grain consequently labour of all kinds must fall, and likewise the price of land must fall in value acording to the prices of Grain, it will severe upon mortgages when estates are dipt(?) which I am doubtful many in Northumberland will be.

Monday 23 — A beautiful fine day at Thornton, to dinner meeting Isaac Milburn.
Tue 24 — A shower of rain, still a pleasant spring, a fine season to sow wheat & beans.
Wed 25 — Sold 27 bolls wheat Mr Blair Abby Mills @ 11/6 weighs 8 – 9.
Thur 26 — At Hartburn Grange Moor, seeing my brother Thomas is poorly.
Fri 27 — A fine Winters day, Mr Watson's Fox hounds at Netherwitton, they killed on Wednesday.

Sat 28	Threshing a wheat stack, bad gift only 30 bolls.
Sun 1	A fine day the grass upon land is quite green, wheat flush.

10th Week March 2 – 8

Such a remarkable fine Winter never known by the oldest person, it has been more like Spring than Winter neither frost nor snow, but fine open and growing season, the Turnips are beginning to flower out in yellow seed, most people is beginning to fear, they will all be spoiled before March is out, the markets for corn are very dull

Wheat fair sample 11/-
Oats fair sample 6/-
Barly " " 7-3
Peas " " 10-6
Beans " " 11-

Mon 2	A stormy kind of day, but still favourable for the Season.
Tue 3	Windy and stormy cold west winds, with frequent showers of Rain.
Wed 4	Hinds hiring a great number of men, delivering 28 bolls of wheat @ 11/6.
Thur 5	Stormy and cold we think of beginning to sow oats.
Fri 6	Threshing oats for seed.
Sat 7	Plowing fallow, delivering 30 bolls of wheat Mr Blair, Abbey Mills @ 11/6.
Sun 8	A fine frosty day expecting to begin sowing oats tomorrow if fair.

11th Week March 9 – 15

The execution of Ralph Joyce is to take place on Wednesday the 18th inst. at Morpeth Goal in front of the Parson, the poor criminal is only 24 years of age, was a hind at Cocklepark under His Grace the Duke of Portland, the charge is Pariside on distroying his fathers life by administering Prusia Acid of which he dies. The evidence was conclusive as he has confessed that he bought the stuff at W. Creighton Chemist Morpeth it has been thought there was a chance of Reprieve but I am Doubtful.

Mon 9	Begun sowing oats, a little frosty, but not to effect the lands.
Tue 10	A fine morning all hands sowing oats 5 harrows in full.
Wed 11	The second days hiring for hinds they are a little higher than last year
Thur 12	Sowing oats, very dry and pining weather.
Fri 13	Sowing oats in the moor, very dry, a shower of Rain.
Sat 14	Windy, threshing oats for seed, and sowing peas in afternoon.
Sut 15	A fine morning wind North, and cold the country is very dry.

MITFORD CHURCH
North.d
Published 1 April 1824, by W. Davison Alnwick

Above – Mitford church 1824. William comments how cold the church was when in this semi-ruined state.
Below – An engraving dating from 1775 of Mitford castle.

MITFORD CASTLE, *in* NORTHUMBERLAND.

12th Week March 16 - 22

The execution of Ralph Joyce took place on Wednesday at 8 o'clock in the morning in the midst of a pitiless shower of hail and snow, about 300 people present, who were all sorry at the disgusting sight of a poor young creature cut down in the prime of life only 24.
It appears he is a very good looking young man, he has made a confession of his guilt, and attributes his fall from a spirit of contention amongst his family and the poison was bought not absolutely thinking to destroy life, but that evil spirit overcome him and so he fell.

Mon 16	Sowing oats day, and works very badly. I hope we shall have more Rain.
Tue 17	Frosty, we got to the field with 15 Bolls of peas and oats, but the harrows did not work.
Wed 18	Joyce the felon execution is to take place this morning at 8 o'clock.
Thur 19	A great snow storm about 15 inches thick, and a severe Frost from the north.
Fri 20	A very frosty, and a great deal of snow upon the ground, a foot and half deep.
Sat 21	A severe cold day and a fall of snow towards noon, threshing peas, very bad.
Sun 22	A frosty morning I should like to see fresh we have part oats to sow yet.

13th Week March 23 – 29

What a favourable fine open winter we have had but now a great change we have had no winterly weather until now, this day, the wind is from the North, and extremely cold.
There is a great quantity of oats to sow all over the country, the Land is got very wet and full of water and a great part of the oats are not finished this has been cast upon the Land, it will do badly should this weather continue, Wheat has got a dashing, it was looking very well till now.

Mon 23	Leading Dung. Preparing for Turnips, stormy and cold.
Tue 24	This day is a little better, not as stormy sold a milch cow @ 16 – 10.
Wed 25	Morpeth horse and cattle Fair, horses are very high, cattle the same.
Thur 26	Sold a 3 year old Quey in milch to John Appleby at 11-10-0.
Fri 27	Banking out Dung for Potatoes and Turnips. stormy and cold.
Sat 28	Threshing oats, cold north wind and showers of Hail and Rain.
Sun 29	A very cold morning, wind in the north, the weather has changed for the worse.

14th Week March 30 – April 5

Three great engagements between our great commander and the Sikhs upon the River Sutlij in India commanded by Governer General Sir. H. Hardage, Sir Harry Smith and General Goff. The first action was a hand fought battle, the second the same and the last by Goff, a final close.
10 thousand kill'd on the enemy side the last battle, and nearly as many before, drove them thro the river Sutlij and drowned thousands. They have sued for peace, with agreeing to pay the expenses of the war, one million and half Sir Hugh is marching upon Lahore, before any agreement, which he is about a days march, he has sent for the inhabitants not to desert the place as protection will be offered.

Mon 30	More likely to be fair, leading Dung. Sold a carving Quey @ 12 – 12
Tue 31	Threshing wheat a stack got inn, before the Rain, expected to be sound.
Wed 1	Rain Rain!! Rain all day, expecting to get on to sow the remander of oats.
Thur 2	A beautiful fine day, after the Rain yesterday. Coals leading and fencing.
Fri 3	Mr Bruntons Mare left after keep since January 10.
Sat 4	A wet afternoon banking out dung for Turnips.
Sun 5	Mr Tindale here at dinner and Mr. W. Coull to tea.

15th Week April 6 – 12

The engagement in India are of a most serious description. Our men went into the enemy intreshment with that vigour as to threating the Sikhs with stagnation, the Battries are stormed and in hand and it was who was to be first into the trenches, quite beyond anything that has been fought in modern times, the Sikhs was commanded by French Officers and showed the most valour and was well supplyd with military stores, much more that we, and had better Cannon. The battle was quite beyond Waterloo for splendor and military glory, I hope it will all settled in peace for many years.

Mon 6	Rain, Rain, Rain, a cold Rain from the North, ewes lambing, got 3 last night.
Tue 7	Rain, cold north another lamb this morning but the land is bottomless.
Wed 8	Paid Mr Wilkinson Bank Agent the poor rate for union first part.
Thur 9	A very frosty morning land is very wet, delivering 52 bolls wheat Newton Mill 13/6.
Fri 10	Rain and very wet weather, Good Friday, ewes lambing got 10.
Sat 11	Plowing up Turnip land, drizzly wet day.
Sun 12	Easter Sunday it is some better this day, but the land wet.

16th Week April 13 – 19

The weather has been most awful of late, ever since Joicey, the convict was hung at Morpeth, we have had a perpitual rain and the sun has never shone since will be 5 weeks since.
There is a large track of land to sow with oats all over the County, many has got very little done. I have about 6 acres to sow and all the turnips land, there has been no plows at work of late and we can scarsley know what to do, expecting threshing you cannot go into the fields without being completely overhead.

Mon 13	Mr and Mrs Wallas here from Blyth & the little boy, Easter Monday.
Tue 14	Threshing a stack of oats, the weather still wet, a great deal of oat land to sow.
Wed 15	Rain, Rain, Rain no looking out, the ewes are lambing, quickly, the poor things are lost.
Thur 16	Rain, Rain, Rain the land completely inundated we can scarsely get out of the house.
Fri 17	Still Rain, can get nothing done, and a great deal of land to sow, with oats.
Sat 18	Rain, Rain, Rain a continuance of wet, the fields bottomless.
Sun 19	Rather better this morning, still the sun does not shine, dull.

17th Week April 20 – 26

It is expected the ransome of the Shiks of Lahore has been paid before this time, one million and half as indemnity, for the expences on the Punjab and Misore teritories. Sir Henry Hardage the Govenor General has provided himself a very clever man and such an officer as England has not had for a serious of time, the military tactics has been quite before Waterloo which is left in the shade. There is a doubt of the Americans going to war with us, for the Oragon territories in the far west – west of the Canada and United Territories.

Mon 20	This day is much better, but the land is very wet, hedging etc.
Tue 21	Begun to sow barley for the first time this season buy, still the weather looks gloomy.
Wed 22	Sold Mr Blair 58 bolls wheat @ 13/6. Rain, still wet weather.
Thur 23	Delivering 58 bolls wheat to Abbey Mills Mr Blair at 13/6.
Fri 24	Rain, threshing a oat stack, Mr Greasons Dancing Party at 7 o'clock.
Sat 25	Rain all work at a stand the land is bottomless the land not sown.
Sun 26	A cold north wind with showers of sleet. I shall gladly see the weather better.

18th Week April 27 – May 3

The season has been the very strangest, that ever was known. We never finished our oat sowing until yesterday 29th. We begun on the 9th March we have never sown any since 16th March, continuously rain every day, and the first sown ones looks very badly. The snails and worms I think have destroy'd them all, being drown'd with continual wet weather. The seasons are quite changd what used to be formerly. I have heard my grandfather say, they had to cease ploughing in the middle of April from severe heat the cattle could not work.

Mon 27	Sowing barley on the Turnip land, but it is very wet, the season is spending.
Tue 28	This day rather better, Doe Hill sale for stock, I hope it will be better.
Wed 29	Sowing barly on Turnip land, sowing the last oats on Clover Lea
Thur 30	This is a fine day, Tranwell sale of stock, plowing fallow.
Fri 1 May	A fine day, a change for the better, we have a long continuum of wet.
Sat 2	Plowing the last of the fallow land, a tollerably fine day.
Sun 3	Drizzly morning and the wind at north east, the moon changes today at 11 o'clock.

19th Week May 4 – 10

The public sales of stock, all over the country, has been very high, Mr Jobson stock at Chillingham New Town has commanded higher prices than I have heard of, Tups and Tup Hogs 16 + 17 Guineas, ewes and lambs 4 Guineas draught horses 50 Guineas, and the milch cows from 25 to 70 Guineas, bulls 30 to 85 Guineas, Calves even at 20 Guineas, 400 sat down to dinner, Loyal & Patriotic Toasts were drank, the Auctioneer Mr James Chrisp officiated, Mr Jobson has been long known as a first rate breader of stock, he now retires into private life.

Mon 4	Carting of Turnips to get the hand sowing with barly.
Tue 5	A great deal of Rain last night, has put us of sowing.
Wed 6	Morpeth Fair for single servants and cattle, I got a man 10£ and a girl 4£ for half year.
Thur 7	Threshing wheat far to the fall, 26 good and 2 backends, prices about 13/-.
Fri 8	Geo. Greason's sale at Park Corner, cattle and joinery and furniture, he leaves for Gateshead Hall.
Sat 9	A fine day, begun sturring Turnips land, a dry day.
Sun 10	Stormy, with wet, bad prospect for the crop upon the land, oats looks badly.

20th Week May 11 – 17

The free trade in corn had passed the House of Commons by a majority of 89, it has to be brought forwards on Monday in the House of Lords, it is expected will pass and what the event will be no one can determine, be as it will the price of grain, must be lower, when it is allow'd from all countries. It is expected the Lords will make a vigorous stand against it but they dare but pass it, the clammer of the people all over is for cheap food. Sir Robt Peel is all for supporting the manufactor, he being one himself.

Mon 11	A very fine day, roling oats they look very badly, paid Mr Reay blacksmith 5-13-0.
Tue 12	Frosty today, rolling Peas, and Oats, and plowing Turnip land.
Wed 13	A thin market at Morpeth, today, a great many flitters, hinds, carts all litterly all places.
Thur 14	Plowing land for Turnips, the wet begins to get partly out of the land.
Fri 15	Frosty this morning, but towards noon, a bright sun.
Sat 16	Delivering 60 bolls oats Coxlodge Colliery, a little frosty this morning.
Sun 17	A disagreeable wet day, Mr Coull here at afternoon.

21st Week May 18-24

The bill has passed the commons for a free importation of corn in to this country, but the Lords appear to set their faces completely against it and it is doubtful whether or not it will pass through the Lords, Sir Robt Peel I think will be ousted as Prime Minister, his calculations in respect of the Corn Traid, has been quite aronious, in the place of the wheat being in May 70/- the best is not more than 56 and some as low as 30/- and yet lower still say 28/- so much for Sir Robt & his predictions.

Mon 18	Rain and a could wind from the east, the season looks very badly, both grass and corn.
Tue 19	Planting potatoes a stormy day, the wind north west.
Wed 20	Sold a milch cow Wm. Coull Esq, £14-10s and her calf, Mr Thos. Blair for 35/-
Thur 21	Sowing clover seed nature windy but the land works well.
Fri 22	Plant, a fine day, men plowing fallow.
Sat 23	Sowing the last of the clover upon the wheat.
Sun 24	A fine morning been a little frosty last night, but fair.

22nd Week May 25 – 31

The Queen is safely delivered of another Princess, she proves a famous breader a most strange weoman no sooner relived from child berth than she is out and planning to be and to some distant nation, it is expected the King of the French, is to visit her in a fortnights time should he not be able, our Queen will pay him a visit or off to Scotland and Ireland. She would like to have Albert to be made King Consort but the nations appear to be totally against it, and very rite, a petty German Prince, penniless to be in such a great nation.

Mon 25	Frosty and very cold plowing fallows, the land works very well.
Tue 26	Assisting Mr Robson Red House. Plowing fallow with 5 plows, dry day.
Wed 27	A cold day and the wind north west.
Thur 28	Our rent day at Mitford, paid Mr Tindall 152£ for H. R. Mitford Esq.
Fri 29	At Middleton giving Mr Coull £60 to purchace sheep at Stagshawbank.
Sat 30	All hands clipping sheep, a fine day, sheared 80 and finished at 6 o'clock.
Sun 31	A bright sun but been frosty last night.

23rd Week June 1 – 7

The Corn Bill for the free admission of grain into this country has passed the House of Lords twice and it is expected will be settled in a weeks time consequently the prices of all kinds of Corn is expected to fall, and it is likewise expected that that land must be taken at 30 per cent lower, and that landlords must submit They have been enjoying much more rent than they were intitled to but I hope the farmers will have their day, as well as they.

Mon 1	At Rothbury Fair, b't [bought] 42 ewes & lambs, Dinmonts 59-8-3, very high market.
Tues 2	A very hot morning yesterday, nearly burnt up in Rothbury hills.
Wed 3	A very hot day, b't [bought] a ton of guanno, Peruvian Willm Pringle at 10£ for Turnips.
Thur 4	A beautiful fine morning, grass and corn has made great improvement.
Fri 5	Tremendious Hot weather, thremomiter @ 120, land extremely dry.
Sat 6	Hot and sultry, working Turnip land, very hard.
Sun 7	A beautiful fine morning, but the weather glass is down two points, change.

24th Week June 8 – 24

The appearance of the weather is much like 1826 that early season when the general election for this county took place at Alnwick and 4 candidates, Lord Howick, Mr Beaumont, Mr Bell and the Hon' H. J. Liddle, I well recollect, the sun was very powerful, the roads were so dusty, it was disagreeable. The wheat harvest commenced in the latter part of July and by all inn by the last week of August, it cannot happen so early this season as the quantity of rain in May remained too long before a change.

Mon 8	Angerton Steads sale by distress, by promisary notes & auctions at law.
Tues 9	Clipping the last of the sheep b't [bought] at Rothbury Fair, Thunder and Rain.
Wed 10	Trinity Wednesday a good many lean cattle shewn & Prices High.
Thur 11	A fine day preparing and plowing the Turnip Land.
Fri 12	Dry weather, the Turnip Land works very dry and without moister.
Sat 13	Roling with the stone roler, the clods are very hard.
Sun 14	Pulled 2 Ears of Wheat in Cop Hills today full out, early season likely.

25th Week June 15 – 21

Sir John Trevelyan of Wallington is no more, he has gone to that born, where no travelor returns. Sir John has been through life a good English Gentleman, very well beloved by all his neighbours and acquaintances. He died at Nettlecombe in Summersetshire, he has been residing there about 3 years, Lady Trevelyan stopping at Wallington, is a pity she had not join'd him her Husband but it appears her voilent Temper forbid it, could we but see ourselves as others see us, it would from many a blunder free us.

Mon 15	At Angerton Steads, sale of stock and furniture, a very high sale, a very hot day.
Tues 16	A very hot day, sowing Turnips, the land is very dry.
Wed 17	Seeing the great show Mr Heughs' splendid carriages drawn by 4 cammels and 2 eliphents.
Thur 18	Thunder but no Rain, sowing Turnips, the land is very dry.
Fri 19	Finished sowing the Turnips, Thunder all day, but no Rain.
Sat 20	Leading Coals for the Tenents, with 5 carts, still very dry weather.
Sun 21	A very hot day, no appearance of Rain, the Corn and Pastures want much.

26th Week June 22 – 28

It is talked in the first rate circles that Mr Robert Peel intends to resine so soon as he can get the free importation of corn into this country, which the farmers dread will be the means of reducing the prices of wheat below the standard, this last year has been ruinous in this part of the world the quallity of wheat has been so very bad and so bad in the gift that it has been ruinious there is not more in each stack, which ought to be double.

Mon 22	Begun mowing new land grass, the great Boat Race at Newcastle for 50£ each.
Tue 23	Newcastle Races begins today, Rain most of day will do a great deal of good.
Wed 24	A windy morning and cold, the weather generally changes at Newcastle Races.
Thur 25	Still unsettled with Thunder in many places the Gold Cup to run for today.
Fri 26	Rain all the afternoon all hands laid of work. The rain will make Turnips grow.
Sat 27	Threshing a stack of wheat this forenoon, men mowing at afternoon.
Sun 28	A fine morning, the weather glass is looking up I hope we shall get hay tomorrow.

27th Week June 29 – July 5

Lord John Russell is sent for by the Queen, to form an Administration in the Place of Sir Robert Peel who has now resined after the free trade in Corn. Earl Gray is in the new Administration and many others of known worth. I should gladly hope they the new ministry will do all the good for the Country the possible can, but I think the Country is not in a very settled state, how the Agriculturist will do, after passing this free trade in Grain, it rather puzzles me.

Mon 29	Stormy and windy weather, mowing and winning hay.
Tue 30	Windy and frequent showers of Rain still we perservere in raking hay.
Wed 1	Gloomy raking hay but Rain at afternoon all hands of at 4 o'clock.
Thur 2	A fine morning I hope it will bring a change of weather to get the hay.
Fri 3	All hands piking hay, put up 43 pikes and a beautiful day.
Sat 4	At Stagshawbank Fair, bought a calving Quey @ 12,5 a very hot day.
Sun 5	A beautiful fine morning and very hot.

29th Week July 13 – 19

The Grand Agricultril Shew at Newcastle takes place this whole Week, Attended by the first Noblemen in the Land. Such a thing I never saw the inside was like a large Town, every Beast, Sheep and Swine were all covered & kept so clean with plenty of Wheat Straw, a refreshing Booth for 300 yards long all covered, the arena consisted of 15 Acres inside, the quantities of Husbandry articles no one could conceive. The Flow(er) Show was splendid with the shew of Fruits outside the incloser was numbers of Inns with every accomodation. I dined in one with some Gentlemen from Fifeshire...

Thur 16 — Attending the Great Agricultral Shew at Newcastle such a thing will not happen again.

Fri 17 — At Thornton seeing W Coull in a poor state of Health, fears of his getting better.

32nd Week August 3- 9

A terable stagnation in the Corn trade, respecting the Duty taken of the foreign Grain, it is most impossible to see old Wheat at any price...

Tue 11 — Paid Mr Mitchell Property Tax,

Landlord	4.8.8
Self as occupier	2.2.7 1/2
Mr Fairfoot	7.6 ½

35th Week August 24 – 30

The wages for Harvest work are very high, on Account of the great demand for the Railway through the east part of Northumberland to Edingborough. I have to give 20/= a week, Victuals & lodging for men and Weomen 16/=

39th Week September 21 - 27

The great failure of the potato crop has become very serious, accounts from all parts are the same. I have taken up a part of mine and they are really very bad when you get one good you will generally get 20 bad, all dun(?) and a kind of blue colour.

Mon 28 — Attending the Magistrates at Tinemouth with W Charlton to arrest Thos & Forster Lonsdale from Crofton House.

Wed 30 — The Barresters day at Morpeth givin inn the lists of Voters & Jury lists return.

42nd Week October 2 – 18

Death of Mr Matthew Reed of Old Town near Elsdon, Aged 25 years he married Miss Jane Bullock of Spittle Hill about 3 years back, it is said he has made too free with the Bottle and has hastened his end...

44th Week Oct 26 – November 1

Terable inundations and Floods in the south of England and Cumberland but particularly in France... ....the low land all under water and coupled with that, the failure of the Harvest and the Potato Crops, that they are on the brink of

Famine. Corn is rison every market day, Ireland is Starving likewise Germany & Poland.

45th Week November 2 - 8

The time of year for a Quittance for given inn for Farms since the Free Trade has become the order of the day. I was yesterday writing to Henry Revely Mitford Esq. Exbury House Hampshire the resignation of my brother Robt. at Newton Park to leave 12 May next 1847 he is very much disgusted from the treatment he received last Autumn in the manners he was treated, after the great improvements he made upon the Farm and the Premises and Fences he cannot think of remaining any longer & rather wishes to go into private life.

Tue 10	Brother Robert giving notice to quit Newton Park Farm on 12 May first.

47th Week November 16 – 22

The Railways are going on through all parts of the Country, this North Berwick is expected to be opened out on the beginning of the year, that line north of Berwick has been in practice for some time, and it is said is a very dangerous line so many curves and turnings upon the Sea Banks…

Wed 17	A fine winter day. Rec.d 10 £ for an old Horse called Lofty, J Appleby.
Sun 22	Had Geo Brewis from Angerton to Dinner.
Thur 26	At Sunderland call'd upon my Tenent Geo Marshal, Rec.d part Rent 5£.

49th Week November 30 – December 6

Ireland seems to be much distressed by accounts from that unhappy Country after all that has been done by England by sending provisions and employing the Popolice in publick works at this time Government has opned out great improvements on purpose to employ but they will not work at 1/6 per Day. Dan O'Connell the great agitator, draws the Rint as is called, that leaves the poor Divils nothing to subsist upon, their Priests has them bound down by superstition to obey!

Tue 8	Paid £5..10s for Half Ton, Oil Cake for Milch Cows, Hoyle & Co.
Sun 13	A great Snow Storm, about 3 foot deep, all stock to hand feed.

52nd Week December 21 -27

Newton Park Farm has been advertised to be Let by proposals which day passed on Tuesday last, and no Offers was made but one Proposal, by an indifferent Tenent, they then applied to my Brother Robt to retake it, not saying at what Rent.

1847

We begin the New Year, with only gloomy forebodings, certainly the prices are very good for all farm produce, but the quantity is considerably short, at what we anticipated, the prospect is bad for the future, this Free Trade will make such a change. It is believed in another year when we will have to contend against the whole World, it must cause a great fall of prices, Northumberland is too high Rented to meet the reduction that is likely to take place and the landlords are a necessiated people they cannot be content without more than the Land will absolutely make, reducing them to peace prices cannot be. Markets are getting higher every market day, the millers are most anxious to buy. The Continent of Europe is short of corn, France, Germany, in fact all excepting America. The only place we can have any supply is mostly from North America. It will take it all to supply all the others, but the next year perhaps will bring round a great supply. They will endeavour to obtain our gold as they are very poor, and like to have our gold.

Wheat at the present ---17/-
Oats 7/6
Barley 10/-

1st Week January 1-3

New Years day, all hands threshing oats for Fodder, not having a single Bottle of straw about the premises. The weather still continues just between fresh and Frost. There are some people at the plow, but few.

Sat 2 A cold stormy day I have had four plows at work today, but we can scarcely get out at the hedges, being so hard blown full of hard snow but it is only for Turnips, which makes us not so much particular.

Sun 3 A stormy morning from the east, with hail and snow and very cold. It rather appears as if it will be another storm of snow. It is so very cold and stormy like.

2nd week January 4-10

The farms are all unlet and are all advertised since the snow. The gentlemen are justly served because they have been robbing the country since 1815, the termination of the FrenchWar. Sir Charles Monck, Belsay, has never had a bid for his and I hope he will have to farm them himself. But all others are the same, Newton Park is given up again at the reduced rent – £200 (the effect of Free Trade.)

3rd Week January 11-17

I have had Mr Tindall here about Newton Park Farm. A person of the name of Dixon, from the Coquet, has (been) bidding them by the Proposal £200 yearly, but has made objections against the cottages and straw sheds, that he has given inn again and now it is advertised again to be let by Proposal The great number of farms still in the newspaper cannot have a bidding. We must all have abatement if possible the first opportunity.

4th Week January 18-24

It appears the farms are likely to be bad to let this season. There has not been one as yet let and a great many more have got into the newspapers this last week. People do not know how to act, this free trade in Corn has made a complete stop to all lettings. The Americans are pouring into this country all the corn ever they can and it is a fortunate thing they have it because all other countries are quite destitute. The prices are still looking up, Wheat is 20/-, Oats 8 to 9/-, Barley 12/-, Peas 13/-, Beans 12/-.

Fri 22 Mr Robert Potts of Rothbury here today. Robert Brewis, Hartlepool and James

6th Week February 1-7

Newton Park is let, at last to Mr Storrer of Brenkheugh ? at the reduced rent of £190. My brother paying at this time £235 yearly, he does not incline to farm any more. He thinks his state of Health is not good and this free trade will make a change of all produce. Great arrivals from America of all provisions, Wheat, Barley and Oats from New Orleans in the Gulf of Mexico, the river St. Lawarance not being navigable until the Spring.

8th Week February 15-21

Died of Thursday last Margaret Fish, a pauper in this township, aged 92. She formerly belonged to Morpeth. Her husband, James Fish, was a weaver. He died about five years ago. She has been kept by her nephew Robert Rodgers, a shoemaker, who was born in this township. He took her after her husband's death. She has been receiving 3/- per week from this township and has left no family.

Sun 21 The funeral of Margaret Fish, a pauper in this township.

9th Week February 22-28

The Farms are still appearing in the Newspapers and cannot be let. Many at very capital places. Ogle Castle and Saltwick, once at a time was let to Mr Coull Esq. At £2,000 yearly. Now I suppose they may be taken at £800 both together, certainly they always was considered very high, and during the French War, when Bonaparte was in his greatest vigour, now this free trade cheques the hopes of the

The restored church seen through the archway of the ruins of Mitford castle c.1900

Tiller of the Soil. There has been large fortunes lost since 1815 by the farmers but I hope they will see the grovelling disposition of the proprietors.

10th Week March1-7

Prepairing to build a house upon the freehold belonging to Mr Fairfoot, in this vilage. It has been a cottage before and I intend lengthing it other six feet and raising the walls two stories, two windows in front and three the upper story and end window in the Gable. I think will be a very pretty house for my Brother Robert to live in after he leaves Newton Park Farm. Fairfoot grants me twelve years leace and pays me £5 per cent for the outlay.

11th Week March 8-14

Still the Farms appear in the Newspapers and a good place this week, a place when there seldom appears advertised, that is Broom Hill, belonging to Earl Grey, near Warkworth, now tenanted by John Swan. I suppose he had not capital to carry on and Earl Grey quitted him. This is the first week it has been in the paper, seldom any of his Lordship's farms are advertised as he lets 21 year leases with an offer at the end of that time, should the tenant survive. It used to be a good place when John Anderson had it.

Sun 14 A dry morning, we get slowly on with the house building on the cottage.

12th Week March 15-21

The Execution of two Criminals at Morpeth on Wednesday at Morpeth Gaol, the two, Matthews and Welsh at 8 0'clock in the morning – was disgusting in the extream, the hangman had not adjusted the rope in a proper way and Welsh rested upon his toes and cryed "Lord have mercy upon me." The hangman then pulled him up and strangled him by pulling at his feet. They had been great savages in their life time and was both found guilty of stabbing with a knife.

Wed 17 The execution of two criminals at Morpeth Gaol this morning at 8 o'clock, George Matthews and James Welsh.

Sat 20 A female child born in this village, William and Margaret Snowdon, dr, Hawdon.

Sun 21 A fine seed morning. I am glad to see such a fine seed time.

13th Week March 22-28

I am building a new house in this village upon Mr Fairfoot's property, he grants a lease of 12 years, and paying me 5 per cent for the outlay. I have got it fit for the timber 28 inst, and I hope we will get it completed in a fortnight time. My brother Robert has to come in on the 12 May, as he leaves Newton Park farm on that day. I am anxious to have it forward as quickly as possible. It will be a fine situation, surrounded by a prity garden.

Fri 26 Leading stones for the building from the River Wansbeck.

14th Week March 29-April 4

The corn markets are up and down every week on account of the great arrivals from America and the Black Sea. Still there seems to be a scarcity all over Europe. Our prices at present is wheat 17 to 18/-, oats 8 to 10/-, barley 11 to 12/6, peas and beans 12 to 14/-, rye 14/-, beef 6 to 7/-, mutton, 6 to 7. Pork 5 to 6/-, bacon 8 to 9/6, butter firkins 58 to 60/-, sweet butter 13 to 14, potatoes 5 to 30/- per load, the greatest price ever known in this county or any other.

Mon 29 Leading slates and laths, water table etc for the new building on Freehold.

Fri 2 Snow, the ground all covered. Stormy weather. At Newton Park.

15th Week April 5-11

We get famously forward with this New House in this Vilage. I have got it all covered inn, I am now busy with the Backchikson [kitchen?] and Pantry & necessary, which is ready for the Timber. It will be a very pretty house and a beautiful prospect to the South, the weather on the whole has been favourable the work has gone on briskly will make the Vilage of Throphill very conspicuous. There are some old houses on this Property require rebuilding, they are likely to fall if nothing is done to them.

Mon 5 Leading Bricks from Morpeth for the new Building, Easter Monday

Tue 6 Sent two times to Belsey Kilns for lime to finish the New House.

16th Week April 12-18

We had a wedding took place on Saturday last at Newcastle. The young lady, Miss Moor, 22/- (?), took flight on the Friday 9th with the Postman to Morpeth and took the train for Newcastle and found the young man about Gateshead, a person of the name of Robson, a shoemaker of Bellingham, and got married. He had been in the habit of harvesting at this place and had a dancing school, a poor look out, she having a fortune.

17th Week April 19-25

We have got the new house upon Mr Fairfoot's property for brother Robert to live in, the first coat of plaster. It looks very well and will be a very pleasant house, of 4 rooms, a pantry and backitchen and necessary surrounded by gardens and will have a fine prospect to the south, to Rivergreen, the Molesdons, Coldsides, Whalton Hill Head, Eddington, Meldon Park and a view to the west, Wallington and the Lease is 12 years with interest for cash expended, from Mr Fairfoot.

Fri 23 Paid Edward Smith, Mr Cookson's servant for 3 acres of Turnips @ £3 per acre, £19 10.

18th Week April 26-May 2

A great number of sales of farm stock and furniture all over this neighbourhood and has been well attended. Work horses are very high. I never remember of seeing horses for husbandry so dear. Nothing under £40, in fact all farm produce sell well, excepting carts, plows and harrows and other traps. People get fanciful and like of work gear better, these are considerations best known to themselves. The plow and the sale may it prosper.

Mon 26 Had the sale of stock at Newton Park. My brother's stock cash £600.

Tue 27 A windy stormy day, plowing fallow, land works well.

Wed 28 Mr Robson's sale of stock at Ogle Castle, the furniture on Friday.

19th Week May 3-9

We had the sale of all the household furniture at Newton Park, belonging my brother Robert. It hapned to turn out a very rainy day, still a great number of people was there and upon the whole the sale passed of as well as could be expected. There was a great number of ladies and not a fue of the male sex, and the biddings was brisk, but people complained of cold and wet, and incessant rain, made it very unpleasant.

Sat 8 The sale of furniture at Newton Park, a very wet day, still a good sale.

20th Week May 10-16

A terrible advance in all the Corn Markets all over Europe, I have bid 25/- for wheat and I am unwilling to take it, I believe it will obtain 30/- before long. America, France, Spain, Germany, Prussia, and Russia are all at starvation prices. I should gladly hope that it may not get higher. Ireland is in a wretched state, great subscriptions are sent from all places to relieve the destitute and dying.

Mon 10 Mr Lenox's sale at Little Callerton, who is declining farming.

Tue 11 Sale of stock at Highland laddie belonging Joseph Arthur.

Wed 12 A wet day, Alnwick Fair day, stock very high both fat and lean.

Thur 13 Had Mr Coull, Ann and George Brewis here this afternoon.

21st Week May 17-23

I hope the wet weather is more settled, it has been quite distressing, the Corn and grass was quite stopped. The oats, in many places are all gone, owing to the snails and other insects. I should think there will be many fields to plow down. The wheat is looking some better. Grass that has been haird(?) is no better than it that has been eat, for no length or substance is in it. This last fortnight all places are swimming. Prices of all grain are on the advance. Wheat at 25 to 28/-

Wed 19	A constant Rain all day, every thing bottomless.
Thur 20	Still rain, the oats are all going off with snails and grub.

23rd Week May 31-June 6

William Coull, our nephew at Thornton, is lying very dangerous ill and it is scarcely expected he will recover of something of a consumption. It is a great pity, he is a very fine young man and just in his prime. His mother is likewise very poorly, but then can nothing better to be expected, she has been long lame and confined to her chair. I hope and trust William will get better, will be very much missed in this part of Northumberland.

Mon 31	Sowing the last of the clover seeds, a beautiful fine day.
Tue 1	Our rent day. Paid Mr Tindall £200 for ½ year's rent due Martinmas
Fri 4	Left for Sunderland to Rec. rents, Pan Lane £13 10, deducting expenses and repairs, £4 3 1½
Sat 5	At Newcastle on my Road home, by Train to Morpeth. Bought 8 barrs iron 3- 3- 17 =@ 14/= 2 14 8

24th Week June 7-13

Sudden changes in the Corn Trade one week up and one week down. Last week it fell 5/- per quarter and this up to 8/-. The millers are completely taken by supprise, expecting the great arrivals from America, but now it has come out there is very little can be expected from the United States or Canada. It is now expected that Russia and the Black Sea will send us succer. It is said a great arrival is on the passage from Oddessa. Yesterday the market was any thing but any samples at Morpeth – scarcely one sample was to be seen.

Fri 11	Died this day W.Coull Esq., Thornton, quite a young man, a Nephew of mine.

25th Week June 14-20

Died on Friday the 11th June, William Coull Esq., of Thornton, quite a young man in the Prime of Life. His illness has been protracted and ended at last in Consumption, just wore out to skin and bone. He is a young man, a Nephew of mine and is much respected, and I believe never injured any person. But in the midst of life we are in death. Awake to righteousness and sin not. Let us eat and drink for tomorrow we die, be not deceived, evil communication corrupt good manners. This I say to you shame.

Wed 16 The funeral of W. Coull Esq., at Thornton. Dined at 2 o'clock, 16 in number besides serv.

26th Week June 21-28

Attending the Remains of W Coull Esq on Wednesday last (16) he was Buried at Hartburn alongside of his Father who was much esteemed, as a true hearted Friend to all, William has died with the same character, as an upright truthful Friend, one who studied to [do] good as much as he could, all the Servants got Morning and appeared absorbed in Grief when the Herse left the place to go to Church, 3 Coaches one Chase and a Herse from Newcastle. Oh, Death, where is thy Sting, Oh, Grave, where is thy Victory.

Sun 27 At Hartburn Grange, spending the Day with Brother Thos. Who is very poorly.

27th Week June 28 – July 4

I intend being at Stagshawbank Fair on Monday, and leaves at 2 o'clock today 4th, to be at Stamfordham all night, will make it easier for tomorrow in a Gig, taking a servant with me to drive the Cattle home, I have sold all my wintering Cattle both Oxen and Queys at an early period, which makes me in want of a fresh lot. I am doubtful they will be bad to purchase, at least those that are very fresh, the severe winter and the failure of the Turnips in spring is the cause of all this.

Mon 5 Bt. 20 Poled Queys Stagshawbank Fair @ 8~15~0 and a Calving Quey @ 10~10~0 = 185~0~0.

Wed 7 The Election of a relieving Officer for the Morpeth Union Mr R. Watson

29th Week July 12 – 18

The Prices of Grain have fallen considerably....but such a difficult Harvest, Corn has come from all places in the Globe, but the greatest is from America, the Yankees have reached very high prices and have plundered our Country of Gold, they will not take our goods in return.

Wed 21 Gooseberry Fair day at Morpeth, a good muster of People made the Market better.

31st Week July 26 – Aug 1

Sir Geo Grey has come forward to canvas the County as Member of Parliament for North North.ld and made a Speach at Morpeth on Wednesday last he is to meet them in Alnwick on Tuesday first being the Nomination Day to meet Lord Osselson & Lord Lovain, I hope the Election will be in favour of Sir Geo, he being a Whig, the other two are Tories. Toryism is become a dead letter, the People are pushing forward to have a change, whether for better or worse.

32nd Week Aug 2 – 8

Married at Meldon Chapel on Wednesday last 4th, Count Maxilian de Mercindfield Brennburg, of Chateau, only Son of Count de Larchanfield, to Emily youngest Daughter of Isaac Cookson Esq of Meldon Park, they intend to go to Bavaria after a little sojurn after Marriage. Mr Cookson has promised a fortune of 10,000 £ but to be settled on herself in case no children. It is thought it very strange Mr Cookson to marry his Daughter to a Foreigner and likewise a Roman!!! Strange things take place.

33rd Week Aug 9 –15

The General Election of North Division of Northumberland, and keenly contested by Sir Geo Grey of Falladon, now Home Secretary for the Home Department, against two Tory Lords, Lord Osselston and Lord Lovain, the Duke of North.ld's Nephew, and was severely contested and won by Sir Geo. the No. are thus at the close

Sir Geo Grey	1366
Lord Osselson	1247
Lord Lovaine	1236

Tomorrow, Friday, I intend being at Alnwick to see Sir Geo Grey fairly chared.

34th Week Aug 16 – 22

At Alnwick on Friday last chairing Sir Geo Grey as Member for North North.ld a very great number of respectable People. Sir Geo made a most beautiful Speach, but Lord Osselston and Lord Lovain disgraced themselves, the former could say nothing the People felt disgraced to him a person, who could not acquit himself at all. The Friends of Sir Geo Lunched at Coxons, the Star, and Lord Fitzclarance late King Wm's Son, made a funny Speach much against the two men defeated, and threw down 300 Guineas as a subscription to assist the expenses.

Wed 18 Attending Morpeth High Church, attending the Visitation as Churchwarden.

35th Week Aug 23 – 29

[*Details of the results of the voting for the regions in Northumberland*]
A complete Victory over the Old Tories in North, and against all the influance of the great Duke & aristocracy of Northumberland.

Thur 26 Newton Park, Sale of Corn, by Mr Sam. Donkin, all Sold, low prices.

Mitford bridge and village c.1900.

Sun 29 A fine morning. Mr Hall and Miss Bab. Coull at Dinner.

36th Week Aug 30 – Sep 5

Brother Robert shifted his Furniture last Thursday to this new House, on Fairfoots Property. The Harvest goes on briskly… Harvest wages from 12 to 15/= plenty of Irish but ungovernable bruits, Pat, is always slovenly and cairless of his togery, many without shoes & not a fue without coats. Poor & Poverty Stricken with all the Money that has been sent into Ireland.

Wed 1 Sep At Morpeth. Hired 6 Men at 12/= per week & victuals.

37th week Sep 6 – 12

The Queens Visit to Scotland, in Steamers round by the Cornwell and western Isles of Scotland, Dumbarton, Inverary, Fort William, Argileshire, Isle of Skye, Taffa and other places, hath given rise to Tourists, many have gone from all places into Scotland lodgins Beds etc have been bad to procure, there has been fine Weather for the Jaunt. I hope the Royal Family will enjoy all the Pleasures.

38th Week Sep 13 – 19

A remarkable fine Harvest… The Irish reapers have been very plentiful and the wages low viz. Men 12 Shillings per week and Countrymen 15/=…..plenty of ragged and Lowsy Irishmen, they left our Beds in a sad state full of living vermin.

41st Week Oct 4 – 10

Mr Robert Hall and I being Executors to the Will of the late Wm Coull Esq, we are obliged to quit the Thornton Farm and have given notice to Mr Snowball the Steward, to that effect. Perhapse Mr Robert will try to take it again, it is a great concern and requires a great attention. Mr Coull enjoys but poor Health at this time but I shall expect he will gather strength, in a little time, ever since he got his Hand shot through with the Gun, his health has been only middling.

43rd Week Oct 18 – 24

A great Failure amongst the Banks at this time, both in London, Liverpool, Manchester in fact all over the Country. Newcastle has come into a share, the Joint Stock Bank and now on Thursday last, the Union Newcastle, Shields & Sunderland, has shaired the same fait. I was at Longframlington Fair on Friday last. I paid away 25 Union Notes, soon the Accts. arrived. I had to fork out Bank of England, it will make a great Stagnation in Trade. I understand it is just the great Failures in the East Indies, and other places.

Thur 21 Our Niece Barbra Brewis of Grange Moor to be married to Mr Stobs Hallowell.

Sat 23 A fine day. Flitting a Tenent into a cottage from Coal Houses, to pay 2 £ on 12 May.

44th Week Oct 25 – 31

The Americans and the Mexicans are at open War, the former have invaded Mexico at Vera Cruse and now have reached the Capital Mexico.... It is too bad one Nation is to over come the other and take possesion of the things that does not belong them...

Sun 31 Mrs Morton, Miss Coull, Richd. Brewis, George Brewis Dined here.

45th Week Nov 1 – 7

A great many Farms have appeard in the public papers and Thornton amongst the rest, I being Executor to the Effects of the late Will.m Coull Esq in duty bound, I was obliged to send the Quitance to Joseph Snowball the Agent for Netherwitton Estate, since then Mr Robt Coull has declined to make them an offer for the farm, hence it appears in the News-papers, they may consent to make him an offer, if not I believe he will decline taken it.

Wed 10 Delivering 10 Poll'd Heifers @ 11 £ each for Berwick, a Mr Wood. Strange to go north.

Sun 14 At Hartburn Grange Moor seeing my Brother Thos who is poorly.

Thur 18 Building a Byre for Brother Robt behind the Cottage occupied by J Robinson.

48th Week Nov 22 -28

They have got our Neighbours Farm, called Throp Hill east Farm, into the Newspapers to let, containing 402 Acres, only in middling condition to be let by Proposals to be delivered to Mr Thos Tindall Newton Underwood on the 2nd December 1847. The term is not specified but it is considered only from Year to Year, it is a very shabby way I should hope people at a distance will be upon their gaurd befor they enter on such a doubtful tenure.

Fri 26 Mr Moors Farm this place is advertised to Let containing 402 Acres.

49th Week Nov 29 – Dec 5

Thornton Farm to Let the day is over, it is reported 900 a year has been offered, but I doubt it very much, Mr Coulls Rent at this time is 750 which I think is quite enough...

Thur 2 Letting day for Thornton Farm. Mr Coull declining taking.

51st Week Dec 13 – 19

Mr Mitchel of Nunriding is to have Mr Moors Farm at 335 £ Mr Moor has not been well treated after paying 370 and then turnd away, at 330 they should have given him a fair chance. Attending the Funeral of the late Mrs Bean, Innkeeper, Morpeth on Thursday. There was not a near Relation there, I had to pay the Expenses there was 3 Chases and a Hearse Mr Charlton Solicitor Dr Hawdon Wm Bean, Casepark (?) & Brother Robt. Her Son William Died about six weeks since.

Sat 25 Christmas Day Mr Potts & Son from Rothbury spending the day.

Tue 28 Angerton Feast day. Dinner at 3 o'clock at Lowangerton and then the Dance at 7 evening.

Thur 30 Snow, about 6 inches thick, it has come in good time not much frost in the ground.

Fri 31 Repairing the Road, leading to Rivergreen Mill in a bad state 2 carts & 3 Men.

[Last page]

This ends the Year 1847 it has been a good Year for me, every thing of farm produce likewise Beef and Mutton have been in proportion good prices.

1848

The Year begins with complaints. Ireland is again in trouble the Manufactories are paying of a great number of hands the Proprietors cannot find Cash to carry on, the great failure of the Banks etc and the great distress amongst all Trades, makes such a depression in all branches of Busness that good men are hardly to be trusted, all confidences are lop'd every one is doubted, the emence Failure that has taken place, many one that have great Capital that has been brought down with others.

Sat 1st Jan Saturday the first Day of the year 1848 A Cold Morning with a little Snow I had a fue Neighbours visiting to Dinner, Mr Thos Bell, Newcastle, Brother Robert, Rich.d Brewis, Thornton, Robt Dixon, Middleton, Mr & Mrs Robson, Red House, Mr & Mrs Robinson of this place, they stop'd for Supper and made very cheerful.

…expecting the bride and groom Mr & Mrs Stobbs, Hallowell, to Dine today on their return home from the yearly Ball at Angerton. They are now on a visit seeing my brother Thomas at Grange Moor who is very poor state of health and I am afraid will never enjoy good health for some time

Week 2 Jan 3 - 9

My Brother Robert and I have been looking at East and Middle Coldsides Farms belonging to Admiral Mitford, we have given in Proposals East 220 and Middle 225 the West Farm has a very bad holmstead, but that will have to be rebuilt, they now are farm'd by Joseph Wilkinson who lives at the East place, there is no time mentioned which is better, now when this free trade is to be tried

Week 10 Feb 28 – Mar 5

A revolution in France & a Proclamation of Republic. Paris has been the scene of Blood and devastation. 500 Men has been Killed in that great City, from last accounts and I am doubtful will be many more. The King has been forced to abdicate and stole away along the Quay got aboard of a steam ship, it is not known where he is gone. England is supposed is the place. His Sons are rejected likewise, the Orleans Family nothing will satisfy but a Republican Government.

Week 11 Mar 6 - 12

Death of my poor Brother Thomas who died on Sunday [5th Mar] at 1 o'clock after a long illness of 6 years standing, at Hartburn Grange Moor, in his 76 year. Has left 5 sons and 4 daughters, all Sons at Home, 2 of the Daughters Married. He has been a real Honest Man through Life and generally beloved and respected by all acquaintances who are very numerous. I would gladly have accompanied his remains to the Grave but extream Illness of a Fevor has left me in a very weak state. 'Where the wicked cease from troubles, the weary are at rest.'

Thu 9th The funeral day of my eldest Brother Thomas, at Mitford, I being unwell could not attend.

Week 13 Mar 20 – 26

Revelutions all through Germany, it appears now that all the Crowned heads throughout Europe is upon the totter, the People sees very plainly that Monarchy is attended with serious expence and every Year is additional, likewise the Bishops and Clargy will fall in for their share, there must be a change in our Exclesiacticks for the better regularly expences the Church is an overgrown Monster and is still adding more Bishops, a thing we can do without.

Sat 1st Apr This is the first fine day we have had for more than 2 Months

Week 15 Apr 3 – 9

The Whole World Revelutionised, and is desirous to follow the same line as France, nothing is heard of but Reform Repeal & Revelution, all thro Germany, Poland, Prusia and Italy, Denmark, all places but England, the Irish is in Rebellion, preparing Guns, Pistols & Pikes, and the most violent Speaches against the present Government, we have certainly got into a bonny mess, with the Expences of the State, and the scarsity of Cash, with the great failures of the Banks, becoming ruinous. The Union Bank Newcastle had made a call of 20 per cent per share.

Sun 16th At Middleton and Grange Moor settling the will of my Brother.

Sat 22nd Mr Mitchells Plows on Mr Moors Farm here today, about 53 Plows.

Week 20 May 8 – 14

Mr Coull has quited Thornton Farm this term and Mr Thos Swan of Morpeth has succeeded at a little more Rent, be that as it would, I am doubtful, Mr Swan will not continue 60 Years upon Thornton like his predecessor. The Netherwitton Landlords has not behaved over well, or at least the Steward, with parting with so good a Tenent, their Rent has been Paid, they may find some difficulty in always finding such like Tenents.

Sun 21st A fine Morning set of to go to the Grange Moor. James has got a broken arm.

Wed 24th A Meeting of the Board of Guardians at Morpeth about building a Fever Hospital.

Thu 1st Jun The wedding day of Ann Brewis of Angerton.

Week 23 Jun 5 – 11

The Irish are crying out for reform and England likewise are meeting in all directions for petition for a remission of taxes & the manufactors for cheap bread & that the Ministry should enforce all Sinecures & Pensions to be reduced and to begin at the Queen and the Queen Dowager particularly she having 100.000 yearly which is thought a disgrace for a single Weoman to have in times of distress when Trades of all kinds are so very bad and the Continent is in complete ferment.

Week 24 Jun 12 - 18

Married at Hartburn Church by Mr Richard Croft, vicar, Lancelot Robson to Ann Brewis, daughter of my Brother Thomas Brewis of Hartburn Grange West Farm on Thursday 1st June and set of for Newcastle that same day to Dine, spent the day in that Town and then arrived at Middleton bank top at 9 the same evening, with George and Hannah her brother and sister.

Thu 17th Aug Mr John Brewis, brewer, here to dine. A fine day.

Mon 21st Valuing the Thornton Crop of Corn for Mr Coull, 350 £

Thu 24th Rain, No attempt to shear. Land is bottomless.

Week 36 Aug 28 – Sep 3

Plenty of Harvest People, the Irish have come over in Shoals, the wages in Ireland is so very low, they have all arrived in England the wages in Kilkenny is just 2d per Day will scarsely keep life in, they are a miserable set of Men, scarsely a rag upon their Backs, Poor megar looking, begarly set, I have this Year engaged young country lads, of good character I am affraid of the Irish, they will do harm before they leave this Country they are so voilent against the English.

Week 41 Oct 2 – 8

We have had the Barrester for the regular lisits of Voters at Morpeth on Thursday, I being Overseer, I objected to Willm & John Moor who left this Township on 12th May last, for which the Barrester scored out, there are none but Mr Fairfoot and I returned for this township of Thophill.

Week 45 Oct 30 – Nov 5

The strangest Weather ever was seen by the Oldest Person living, since 28th Aug intill this present day 5 Nov scarsely a fair day we had 3 weeks fine at the beginning of Harvest but after that nothing but Rain and Snow, the great Commit that appear'd in the months of Aug, Sep & Oct must made a change in the Weather altogether it must had great influance on the planitary sistem, should it not take up soon, will be a total Ruin.

Sun 5th A severe Frost all locked up, no wheat will be sowing. Ruin!!!

Thu 9th	Sowing Wheat amongst the clarts and wet, no appearance of better.
Fri 24th	Sold a Brown Horse Tigar to Mr John Appleby, Abby Mills 10 £
Sat 25th	A frosty day. Bathing the Ewes & Hoggs to prevent the Itch.
Sun 26th	Found this morning a Grey Mare of mine in a Drain. Dead, a great loss.
Tue 12th Dec	Mitford Association held at W Thompson the Plow Inn. 18 Members, I, Treasurer.
Wed 13th	Making out the list of the Members, to put in the Hue & Cry and Chronicle.

Week 52 Dec 18 – 24

Strange!! The Pope of Room is absconded from his dominions into Cicly from Revelution in Italy, the great Infalable Pope, the Person who holds the Keys of Heaven and Hell, if he be infallible why fear Man, when he has their Souls a keeping and can grant absolution to Man, and clear him from all his Sins, but I hope and Trust, that the People will never again be gull'd by superstition and bigotry with such false Profits!!!

Sun 24th	At Stannington Vale seeing my Sister Coull who is poorly.
Sun 31st	A calm Frosty Morning the last day of the Old Year. Amen.

1849

Sunday 14th January: Attending the funeral of my much esteemed friend John Brewis, Brewer of Morpeth, aged 40, a most excellent Tradesman and has left a family of 8 children, the eldest boy only 14… ...paul bearer at 3 o'clock, a young man 40, cancer of the bowell.

Sat 3rd Feb Ellen [*William's housekeeper*] has heard her sister Mrs Reid in London is found dead in bed.

Week 7

Died at Whittingham on Wednesday 7 February John Carnaby Esq our cousin, my mother and his mother were two sisters. They left Todburn and went to Shawdon House, Ralph his brother died there about 5 years ago, neither married. Mrs Donkin at Shawdon likewise, Mrs Collin at Sunderland, Mrs Donkin had a daughter and was killed by lightning when standing in the kitchen preparing to go to a sale of furniture. Strange as it may appear, it is said he has left his property which is said 15 or 20,000 to Dr Trotter of Morpeth, should it be so, it is said he was not capable of making his will but the Dr had haunted him to settle his affairs upon the Hargrave family of Shawdon, how that may be time will determine, he has no relative but our family and more strange, never sent word he was dead, or invited to his funeral!!!

Wed 21 Feb Sister Coulls funeral at Stannington Vale, left at 12 & arrived @ Hartburn 3.

Week 9

Died at Stannington Vale, my sister Coull, late of Thornton, in her 78 year, and was buried at Hartburn on Wednesday 21 inst. greatly respected. Few friends was invited, has left 3 brothers, James, Robt and myself. Few have gone to the grave more beloved by all ranks of society, she was generous, open and a great flow of spirits, about 12 followed to the interment. Likewise died at Blyth Mrs Graydon 16 Feb, my brother James wife's mother belonging Newcastle. I had likewise to attend that funeral but could not attend

.

Fri 2nd Mar. Died at Stannington Vale yesterday at 2 o'clock Mrs Murton, widdow of W Murton.

Sat 3rd Mar. Had Mr Coull here settling about Mrs Murton's funeral which is fixed Monday.

Week 10

Death!!! I have to record the Death of my niece Mrs Murton, now of Stannington Vale, Daughter of Mrs Coull late of Thornton who died only a fortnight ago. Mr

Murton was Head Agent to Lord Ravinsworth and Partners called the Grand Allies Collieries, a very clever man who died a few years ago at Newcastle. It is melancholy to think of so many Deaths amongst our friends of late and God knows how soon we likewise may be called upon to give an account at the throne of Grace.

Mon 5th Mar. Funeral day of Mrs Murton, got the Cambo Chase arrived at Stannington Vale at 10 o'clock and sett of for Newcastle at 1/2 past twelve, arrived at St Nicholas Church at two, the remains deposed beside her husband.

Fri 4th May At North Middleton Dining with Mr Coull and arranging matters with Mrs Brewis of Grange Moor.

Week 22

An alarming & destructive fire took place at Shawdon Hall, the seat of W Pawson Esq on Sunday last, it is supposed from some person leaving a smoking pipe of tobacco in one of the stables, they got the horses & carriages out but a great deal of damage done to the buildings, likewise the Manor House all the lead of the spouts was running down the walls. But the Hand of Providence is sure and retribution cometh in due time, the family Dr Trotter & Mr Smart of Sunderland swindled our family of the cash and goods belonged our cousins Carnabys effects!!!!

Week 24

The French and the Italians have had several engagements at Roam but the Italians have got the better, have beat them back from the city but the French begin to be ashamed of themselves to declare themselves Republicans and to force the Pope to remain amongst the people when they do not want him, is cruel in the extream, but all the Continent of Europe are in arms, for a change for their rights, and why should they not have them.

Thus 14th Jun. The Stockton Otter Hounds in this water, had a fine run and kill'd in my West Haugh. About 60 people were there.

Week 30

It is reported here that one of my Nephews is Dead at Southport near Southampton but I have not heard from my brother James, he being the eldest son, a shipwright there. He married a Leutenant of the Navy's widdow about 3 years ago, such is the fate of all humans, we spring up to be cut down in the prime of life. The young may die, but the old must. Nothing so uncertain as life of man, he groweth up and is cut down as a flower.

Week 31

I have to announce the Death of my nephew Thomas Brewis, who died at Gosport, near Portsmouth last week very suddenly from Cholora. He wrote to his parents at Blyth last Monday and was a corp[se] on the Tuesday night. He was a shipwright at that place, he married a Leutenant in the Navy about 4 years ago Widdow with 3 children of her own, he having 3 by a former wife, Miss Purvis, Alnwick, poor fellow a fine looking man, and eldest son of Brother James.

Week 41

Cholera is still raging in some parts of the Country, at Alnwick it has been very bad as many as 17 funerals in one day, which is awful in such a small place. Thank God we are blessed with good health in this place, we have 4 cases this Harvest, 3 Irishmen and a servant boy, John Richardson. A purging and vomiting and Ellen gave a spoonful of the best Turky, Rubarb, two spoonfuls of spirit and sweet nitre with a glass of brandy and invariably had a good effect. The Doctors have been much in the dark, they having give Calomal and Opium (?) which has been too severe and the patients have almost all died, the poison rests upon the stomach.

Fri 26th Oct. Ellen and her sister Isabella at Longframlington at their brother Isaac.

End of 1849

Christmas has passed away in but a dull manner to what I have seen in my younger days!!! I have seen in my youth a few friends amusing themselves until after the New Year sporting with the gun or hunting with the hounds. Old W Bullock, Spittle Hill, about the year 1789 met all of us young people at that time and spend the Hollidays mostly at Throp Hill and many was the pleasant Days I have spent which when I look back appears a Dream, now old age creeps on apace.

1850

1st Jan Now begins the year 1850. I can well recollect when a boy at school of writing 1788 when at Hartburn School teached by Joseph Reed, Clark and School Master it is many long years since that time, but when I look back what strange occurances has hapened since then and how strange everything appears, and how times has changed. I think considerably worse, the people have changed as well as times, there is nothing like the Honesty and Stability that was at that time. Men care nothing about Honesty now, Bankruptcy and Defraud.
England, I am sorry to say has got into nothing but confusion, all trades & farming are become so bad with low prices that it appears like nothing but a National Bankruptcy. Low prices of farm produce have caused such a gloom over all the country. Nothing but political meetings all over the country before the meeting of Parliament, some for Free Trade and others for Protection duties, say 8/- per Quarter upon all foreign wheat and other grain in proportion. Parliament meets upon the 31 of this month. I expect there will be great changes, England is in a most ruinous condition with the National Debt coupled with useless Pentioners of no earthly good and the Established Church which is as great an evil as any, 10 millions yearly, great shame eating up the vitals of the state.

Wed 9th — Mr Coull called to sign a petition for a protection duty upon Corn.

Mon 14th — There is a great thickness of snow. The sheep can get nothing but what is given them; Turnips or hay and the fodder is not plentiful.

Thu 17th — A meeting of farmers and others to sign a petition to Her Majesty for protection for agriculture.

Thus 24th — Very unwell taking a little opening medicine to carry off the dizziness in the head.

Fri 25th — I have sent for Dr Hawdon, He came at 5 o'clock and let blood in both arms.

Sat 26th — I feel a little better the affection of the head is much abated, still languid and weak.

Sun 27th — A fall of snow with a severe frost all night. Everything must have Turnips or Hay.

After this the entries become sporadic, not daily as in all other diaries. Then another hand takes over some of the daily accounts of farm activities and later still, many entries are in pencil in a third hand. These deal with minor accounting such as paying off farm workers - by the day rather than six-monthly or yearly as in the past. It seems somebody is looking after the day-to-day running of the farm - perhaps one of the brothers? William died of Pleuro-Pneumonia on 31st January.

ERECTED
To the memory of
Thomas Brewis
of Throphill
who died May 31st 1809 aged 72 years
Margaret
his wife died Jany 24th 1824 aged 82 years
George
their son died July 10th 1795 aged .... years
Richard
their son died May 3rd 1824
Margaret
their granddaughter died ....
aged 10 years
William
their son died Jany 31st 1850 aged 71 years
Thomas
their son died March 9th 1848 aged 76 years
Hannah his wife died March 26th 1855
Aged 80 years

Inscription on the Brewis family headstone at Mitford church

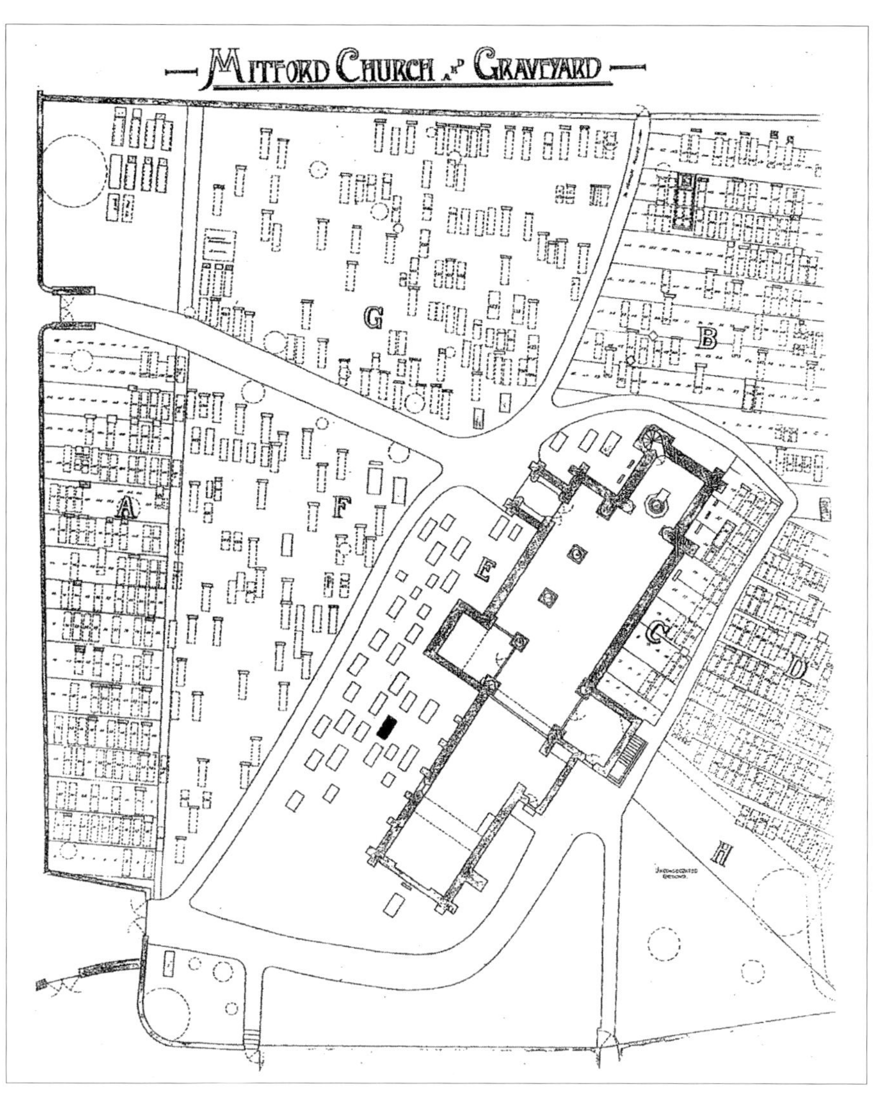

The Brewis Family headstone is marked in black on graveyard plan above

The Brewis headstone in the foreground

Glossary

anker	a measure of alcohol
boll	a measurement of corn, wheat etc.
bondager	a farm worker, usually female, often employed alongside a male hind.
carlings	fried grey peas eaten on Carling Sunday.
Chartists	supporters of the parliamentary reform movement of 1837-48 ; known as The Peoples Charter.
crack	chat, conversation, news etc.
deaf stint	plot of poor land given to workers for their own use.
flitting	moving furniture and belongings to a new home usually in connection with new employment.
fold	a pen or enclosure for livestock (pinfold).
fother	a fother of lead = 21cwt (a cart load).
gift	yield of a crop
hind	a farm servant, usually a married ploughman.
hirings	a fair or market at which country servants are hired.
hovel	a small poorly built dwelling.
lea	grassland, meadow, pasture.
pining	to impound stray animals/ put into a pinfold.
poke	a sack or bag
quey	a cow or heifer in calf
thrave	a number of sheaves or bundles of corn.
throng	busy
toggery	clothing

More books of local interest from Wagtail Press

Memories of Hexhamshire

Hexham Remembered

The Life & Times of Thomas Dixon 1805-1871

Whitley St. Helen's Churchyard, Hexhamshire

Homecoming (poems by Wilfrid Gibson)

Golden Days (a Corbridge childhood)

Further details from Wagtail Press
www.wagtailpress.co.uk
wagtailpress@yahoo.co.uk
Mail order available

Wagtail Press